Domestic Taxation and Foreign Trade

Michael von Steinaecker

Domestic Taxation and Foreign Trade
The United States-European Border Tax Dispute

Praeger Publishers New York Washington London

PRAEGER SPECIAL STUDIES IN INTERNATIONAL ECONOMICS AND DEVELOPMENT

PRAEGER PUBLISHERS
111 Fourth Avenue, New York, N.Y. 10003, U.S.A.
5, Cromwell Place, London S.W.7, England

Published in the United States of America in 1973
by Praeger Publishers, Inc.

© 1973 by Praeger Publishers, Inc.

Library of Congress Catalog Card Number: 72-83010

Printed in the United States of America

To Marina

Border tax adjustments for internationally traded goods are a subject of international controversy. The soundness of the respective rules in the General Agreement on Tariffs and Trade (GATT) has frequently been challenged, and even those who accept the rules disagree on their interpretation. The views of the United States and the European Economic Community concerning this issue are opposed. Thus, the border tax problem is one aspect of the confrontation between these two powers in matters of trade and monetary policy, which, in turn, is only a part (though an important one) of the far-reaching struggle over the distribution of political influence and leverage in the Western world.

One aim of this book is to contribute to the discussion concerning the taxation of internationally traded goods and thereby to aid in the search for a rational solution of the dispute.

However, the book proposes to serve further and broader purposes. The border tax problem is of interest beyond the political significance of the present controversy in that it touches on a variety of basic questions in the field of foreign trade policy. Consequently, many of the considerations and thoughts expressed in the following pages are applicable to other transnational issues as well. The inquiry is intended to contribute to an understanding of the range of questions at the core of many of the more particular problems of international economic regulation.

In at least two respects, the subject of this book is a paradigm of commercial policy issues. First, a focal point is the degree to which international regulation should restrict the freedom of participating nations to pursue economic and social policies of their own choice. Therefore, much space is devoted to the general question of how to compromise conflicting national and transnational policies. Second, the border tax dispute straddles the two fields of economics and law. This made it necessary to consider in this book general problems of drafting, interpreting, and enforcing trade agreements such as GATT and at the same time to evaluate the role of economic theory in the interpretive and regulatory process. In addition, a particular effort has been made to define the businessman's concept of fair international competition (which is frequently adopted by government policy-makers) and to demonstrate its values as well as its fallacies.

The scope of this study is not, however, limited to transnational questions; the work provided the opportunity, which the author willingly accepted, of dealing with some of the legal, economic, and political forces shaping national tax laws.

This study is a heavily revised version of the author's dissertation (Doctor of the Science of Law, Cornell University, 1971). Large parts of Chapters 3 and 6 have been written anew, and numerous changes have been made in other chapters as well.

I gratefully acknowledge the support of John J. Barceló of the Cornell Law School faculty, who contributed a great many comments and suggestions from the very beginning of the investigations to the final revisions. I am also much indebted to Ian R. Macneil (Professor of Law at the University of Virginia) and Paul M. Hohenberg (Professor of Economics at Cornell University), who read the manuscript and gave me the benefit of their criticisms and suggestions. In addition, I received assistance from Jay Levin, in his capacity as Assistant Professor of Economics at Cornell University.

Michael von Steinaecker
June, 1972

Page

PREFACE   vii

PART I: UNITED STATES VERSUS EEC:
DEVELOPMENT AND SIGNIFICANCE
OF A TAX DISPUTE

Chapter

1   THE EVOLUTION OF TWO DIFFERENT TAX
     SYSTEMS   3

     Direct Versus Indirect Taxes: A Century of
       Tax History   3
       The Present Pattern: Two Different Tax
         Systems   3
       The Evolution of the Progressive Income
         Tax   4
       The Triumphant Advance of the Turnover
         Tax   4
       Outlook   7
     Border Adjustments for Domestic Indirect Taxes   8
       A Long-established Practice   8
       Confirmation by International Law   9
       Uncertainty and Vacillation: The Scope of
         the Border Adjustments   9
     The Culprit of the Tax Dispute: The Value-added
       Tax   10
     Breakdown of the Cumulative Turnover Tax and
       Rise of the Value-added Tax: The Example of
       West Germany   11
       A Changed Political Scene   11
       Border Adjustments and the EEC Court of
         Justice   12
       Competitive Neutrality and the West German
         Federal Constitutional Court   13

Chapter   Page

      The Proliferation of the VAT in Recent Years   14
        Tax Harmonization in the EEC   14
        The Spread of the VAT to Countries Outside
          the Common Market   17

2   THE TAX DISPUTE   19

      The Background: The Deficit in the United States
        Balance of Payments   19
      The Challenge: United States Arguments Against
        the Present Border Tax Adjustments   20
        An Attempt to Classify the Arguments   20
        The Businessman's View: Unfairness   21
        The Economist's View: Disregard of Modern
          Economic Theory   23
        The Lawyer's View: Violation of GATT   27
        The Government Representative's View:
          Changed Circumstances   28
      The Threat of Action: The United States Arsenal
        of Trade Weapons   29
        Multilateral Action   29
        Unilateral Action   30

        PART II: THE POLICY ISSUE: HOW
    SHOULD DOMESTIC TAX LAWS DEAL WITH
      INTERNATIONALLY TRADED GOODS?

INTRODUCTION: IN SEARCH OF POLICIES   35

3   ECONOMIC EFFECTS OF BORDER TAX AD-
    JUSTMENTS ON WORLD PRODUCTION AND
    WORLD TRADE   38

      Border Tax Adjustments and Economic
        Efficiency   38
        Economic Efficiency   38
        General Indirect Taxes   44
        Selective Indirect Taxes   51
        General Direct Taxes   53
        Selective Direct Taxes   54
      Tax Changes and the Balance of Payments   55
        The Policy Goal: Independence of the Balance
          of Payments from Domestic Tax Changes   55

Increase of a General Indirect Tax   60
Increase of a Direct Tax   61
Tax Decreases   62
Substitution of an Indirect Tax for a Direct
Tax   62
Indirect Taxation and International Factor Move-
ments   63
Definition of the Issue   63
International Factor Movements Caused by the
Levy/Subsidy System of the Destination
Principle   67
Preliminary Conclusions   68
The VAT and Other General Indirect Taxes   68
Selective Indirect Taxes   69
General Income Taxes   73
Selective Income Taxes   74

4   THE ECONOMIC ISSUES IN THE BORDER TAX
DEBATE: AN ATTEMPT AT CLARIFICATION   76

The Tax Shifting Controversy and the Border
Tax Problem   76
Tax Shifting and Economic Efficiency   77
Tax Shifting and the Balance of Payments   78
"Trade Diversion" and "Trade Distortion"   81
Fair International Competition   83
The Businessman's View of Unfairness   83
International Cost Comparisons   86
Government Interference I: Taxes   88
Government Interference II: Activities That
Reduce Business Costs   89
Government Interference III: Implementation
of the Destination Principle   91
The Concept of Tax Neutrality   93
Domestic and International Neutrality   93
Neutrality With Respect to the Balance of
Payments   93
Neutrality With Respect to International Trade
and the International Division of Labor   94

5   BORDER TAX ADJUSTMENTS AND NATIONAL
    TAX SOVEREIGNTY   98

    Should International Law Limit the Tax Power
      of the State With Respect to Internationally
      Traded Goods?   99
        Conflict Between the Fiscal Sovereignty of
          Different States   99
        Conflict Between the Tax Power of a State
          and the Economic Interests of Other
          States   101
    Destination Principle Versus Origin Principle:
      Which Interferes Less With National Tax
      Sovereignty?   102
        Raising of Revenue by Means of Selective
          Indirect Taxes   102
        Taxation as an Instrument of National Policy   104
        A Practical Example: Italy in August 1970   108
    Taxation of Internal Trade in Federations:
      Model Solutions for World Trade?   108
        Taxation of Interstate Commerce in the
          United States   108
        Taxation of Intracommunity Trade in a
          Future United Western Europe   112
        Model Solutions for World Trade   113
    Final Conclusions   114
        Origin Principle Versus Destination Prin-
          ciple: Policy Conclusions   114
        Border Tax Adjustments and Other Levy/
          Subsidy Systems Distinguished   115

            PART III: THE PRESENT INTERNATIONAL LAW
                    OF BORDER TAX ADJUSTMENTS

6   THE RULES ON BORDER TAX ADJUSTMENTS
    IN THE GENERAL AGREEMENT ON TARIFFS
    AND TRADE: INTERPRETATION AND CRIT-
    ICISM   121

    Introduction   121
        The Pattern of Border Tax Adjustment Rules
          in GATT   121

The Geographical Expansion of the GATT
Tax Law   121
Interpreting the GATT Rules on Border Tax
Adjustments   122
Border Adjustments for General Taxes   124
Border Adjustments for General Indirect
Taxes   124
Border Adjustments for General Direct
Taxes   128
Border Adjustments for Selective Taxes   131
Border Adjustments for Selective Indirect
Taxes   131
Border Adjustments for Selective Direct
Taxes   132
Violations and Remedies   133
Remedies Available to States   133
Remedies Available to Businessmen   134

Appendix   137

I   MAXIMIZATION OF PRODUCTION VERSUS OPTI-
MIZATION OF TRADE: A COMPROMISE SOLU-
TION FOR SELECTIVE INDIRECT TAXES   136

II   THE RULES ON TAXATION OF INTERNATIONALLY
TRADED GOODS IN THE GENERAL AGREEMENT
ON TARIFFS AND TRADE (GATT)   145

NOTES   149

SELECTED BIBLIOGRAPHY   167

ABOUT THE AUTHOR   170

UNITED STATES VERSUS EEC: DEVELOPMENT AND SIGNIFICANCE OF A TAX DISPUTE

**THE EVOLUTION
OF TWO DIFFERENT
TAX SYSTEMS**

DIRECT VERSUS INDIRECT TAXES:
A CENTURY OF TAX HISTORY

The Present Pattern: Two Different Tax Systems

The basic reason for the tax dispute that will be the topic of the following chapters is the fact that the main protagonists in this dispute, the United States on the one side and the countries of the European Common Market, or European Economic Community (EEC), on the other, use different methods to extract taxes from their populations. The fundamental difference between the tax structures on the two sides of the Atlantic Ocean is this: Whereas the United States relies heavily on direct taxes* and uses indirect taxes only as a relatively minor,

---

*The terms "direct" and "indirect" taxes are used here with the following meaning. Indirect taxes are all taxes that are levied against goods and services and thus only "indirectly" on people. Usually they are computed as a percentage of the price of the respective good or service. Turnover and sales taxes of any kind and excise taxes are the main examples. Direct taxes are all taxes levied directly on persons (legal or natural), especially income or profits taxes. This distinction between direct and indirect taxes rests on a formal criterion, the method of computing the tax, and disregards (1) the tax incidence, and (2) the legal meaning these terms may have in a particular statute, e.g., the U.S. Constitution. All other taxes, e.g., property taxes, belong to a separate third group. Inasmuch as they are generally not very important in any country's budget and as their influence on international trade in goods is minor, they are neglected in the following considerations.

supplementary source of revenue, especially on the state level, the
EEC countries on the average get more than half of their total tax
revenue from indirect taxes.[1] Among these indirect taxes, general
turnover taxes are more important than special excise taxes.[2] The
fact that the total tax burden, expressed as a percentage of the gross
national product (GNP), is considerably higher in the EEC than in the
United States,[3] adds to the difference between the levels of indirect
taxes. As a result, indirect taxes are much higher in the EEC than in
the United States.

    This difference is the basic source of all the problems that today
arise in the taxation of internationally traded goods. It is, therefore,
important to understand its causes. It is not, like tariffs, quotas, or
levies on agricultural goods, a shrewd invention of protectionists in
Europe but the result of a long historical development that had nothing
to do with foreign trade. The following discussion will show that the
last one hundred years have witnessed two major evolutions in the field
of taxation. Like all other countries, the United States heavily participated in the first, but, contrary to the countries of the European Continent, it kept more or less aloof from the second, and this offers the
basic explanation for today's difference between the tax systems on
the two sides of the Atlantic Ocean.

The Evolution of the Progressive Income Tax

    During the nineteenth and early twentieth centuries, the pro-
gressive income tax superseded the ancient tax systems to a larger
or smaller extent in all modern states.[4] Among the many reasons
two are conspicuous. The vast development of commerce and stock
companies was accompanied by new kinds of income, independent from
"real" objects such as land and property which for centuries had
provided the main tax base; this alone would have attracted the attention of the state, always in search of new sources of revenue. A
concomitant political philosophy of social justice, teaching that everyone should support the state according to his personal financial ability,
accelerated the changeover from a tax system focusing on objects to
one focusing on persons. Great Britain and Prussia introduced tax
systems remotely akin to the modern income tax as early as around
1800. With the extension of the income tax to corporations, its advance
and spread to all modern countries became all the more triumphant.
Resistance against the income tax in France and in the United States
developed into famous chapters in the political and legal history of
these countries. As the two last states in the Western world to do so,
they introduced a progressive income tax in 1913 and 1914, respectively.

The Triumphant Advance of the Turnover Tax

The Turnover Tax: A Child of the War

The turnover tax (a tax levied on businessmen which is computed
as a percentage of their turnover[5]) can be traced back to the first
centuries B.C., but it had long been neglected in modern nations. The
enormous financial pressure experienced by European countries during
World War I suddenly revived it. Germany introduced a limited form
in 1916 and extended it to a comprehensive turnover tax in 1918.
Following the example of what was then her foe, France began to levy
a similar tax in 1917. Italy followed suit in 1919. Within the next
three years, Czechoslovakia, Belgium, Hungary, the Soviet Union,
Luxembourg, and Austria adopted the new tax. The rates were low—
very low compared with today's turnover taxes. For instance, the
comprehensive German tax of 1918 was levied at a rate of 1 percent
on every transaction.

The Exhaustion of the Income Tax

The turnover tax was not just a new means to finance a war, as
might appear from the foregoing paragraph. Rather its introduction
was a logical and reasonable step in European tax history—a fact
which is proved by its extraordinary development during the following
decades, which would certainly not have occurred if the new tax had
been nothing more than a wartime emergency measure.
    The ever-increasing financial need of the state, especially
during World War I, led to exploitation of the income tax almost to
its limits. This was felt in two ways: not only were the marginal tax
rates increased for the highest incomes, but taxation of lower incomes
was introduced and extended. For two reasons, this development paved
the way for the turnover tax.
    With the change of the personal income tax from a "rich man's
tax" to a "people's tax" it is in danger of losing its main political and
social purpose: the favoring of the "poor" over the "rich," which once
had made it so attractive. The corporate income tax does not remedy
the situation; there can be little doubt that at least a part of this tax
is shifted forward into prices and is thus paid by the consumer. It
could even be argued that more than anywhere else this shifting occurs
in the case of food and other necessities of life, where the elasticity
of demand is very low.[6] If this were true, the corporate income tax
would tend to hit the poor with special severity. On the other hand,
the turnover tax (or any other indirect tax, for that matter), long
denounced as being regressive and therefore unacceptable for social
reasons, allows discrimination between necessary goods and others.

Indeed, many countries today do exempt food from turnover taxes or apply a lower rate. One could easily conclude that it would be better for social reasons to introduce an indirect tax with some differentiation, especially for food, than to exploit the personal income tax up to the point where it becomes a mass tax or to increase the corporate income tax beyond a certain limit.

The second reason why the use of the income tax is limited is not a social but a psychological one. Direct taxes have a bearing on individual effort, difficult as this is to ascertain. Indirect taxes, in contrast, leave the businessman with the impression that he can pass them on to the purchaser. Given, in addition, their broad inclusion of every transaction, they invoke less tax resistance and tax evasion. This may prove to be an invaluable advantage over a direct tax.

The First Half Century of the Indirect Tax

Having realized that new tax sources could only be opened up in the field of indirect taxation, the countries of the European Continent did not hesitate to use the new instrument. Some countries—for example, Italy and France—even began to favor it over the income tax. The turnover tax proved to be a rather stable source of income in times of economic crisis and inflation. Many considered it to be more neutral toward business than the progressive income tax which penalizes successful and efficient businesses. By the time World War II broke out many European countries already had fairly high turnover taxes. The financial pressure most countries experienced during and in the wake of that war led to a further advance of the new tax. Countries such as Sweden, Switzerland, and Great Britain had to give up their resistance and adopt indirect taxes. In Germany, where the turnover tax had been increased from 1 percent to 2 percent in 1922 and had not exceeded that rate for more than two decades, the Allied Powers in 1946 set a new rate of 3 percent in an effort to overcome the desperate financial need of the Länder which had succeeded the vanished Reich. After the Federal Republic of Germany was established, the rate was raised to 4 percent. In view of the current tax controversy it is not without some irony that, again, the United States was a major force in bringing about that increase: the extension of a dollar credit needed very much by West Germany in 1951 was (understandably) conditioned upon a substantial tax rise. As in the case of World War I, almost all of the newly introduced or increased taxes remained in effect even after the financial impact of the war gradually had subsided.

The Case of the United States

In a development in the United States quite similar to that going on in Europe, the Depression of 1929-30 forced many states to introduce turnover taxes in the form of sales taxes. The importance of state sales taxes has grown continuously since that time.[7] But on the federal level the United States has never introduced a general turnover tax,* and the bulk of the total revenue is still received from direct taxes. The income tax system is not yet exhausted. True, the United States income tax has—just like the European income taxes—developed into a mass tax.** But the "psychological breaking point" was experienced by European countries as early as in World War I—the point where new financial needs call for new taxes and a further extension of the income tax seems impossible—has not yet been reached in the United States.

The United States is a country with relatively high incomes. In order to produce a given tax revenue per capita, the ratio of the total tax burden to national income can be smaller than in countries with a lower income level. And a look at the statistics shows that this ratio in fact is considerably smaller in the United States than in the EEC.[8] Therefore it is still possible for the United States to rely mainly on direct taxes.***

Outlook

It is tempting at this point to speculate about future developments. Such thoughts are directly related to the present tax dispute. If the tax systems on both sides of the Atlantic Ocean were to become more similar than they now are, the main reason for the present difficulties would dwindle.

The advance of the indirect tax in European countries described in the foregoing paragraphs need not continue; these countries are now able to broaden the income tax base to an extent not possible in the past. This is mainly due to the increasing significance of corporations in their economies and the concomitant decrease in the number

---

*There are only a few selective federal excise taxes, which are not very significant in the federal budget. As to the proposals for a United States value-added tax, see text, Chapter 2, "Adoption of the VAT in the United States."

**In the first years of its existence, the number of the annual tax returns was 4 million; ten years later it had increased to 7 million; in 1942 it reached 27 million—a vivid illustration of the continuous broadening of the tax base and erosion of tax exclusions.

***Another reason may be that in countries with a strong democratic tradition personal income taxes have deeper roots and greater psychological justifications than elsewhere.

of self-employed businessmen. It is unlikely that Western Europe's
tax systems, even in the case of highly socialized nations, will develop
toward the striking preponderance of turnover taxes observed in the
communist countries, especially the Soviet Union, where turnover
taxation is by far the most important source of income of the state.[9]
The ratio of direct taxes to indirect taxes in European countries may
well remain stable in the decades ahead.

The present gap between the tax systems would, therefore,
probably become smaller if the United States should finally join in
the second development of the last century's tax history, i.e., rely
increasingly on indirect taxes.

BORDER ADJUSTMENTS FOR DOMESTIC INDIRECT TAXES

A Long-established Practice

The existence of two different tax structures does not in itself
suggest any problems for international trade. But for as long as indirect taxes have existed they have been accompanied by "border tax adjustments," i.e., special tax measures for international traded goods.[10]
These adjustments sought to ensure that imported goods bore the same
tax burden as domestic goods and that exported goods bore no tax burden at all. Fiscal measures of this kind put into effect what is known
as the "destination principle," i.e., internationally traded goods are
subject only to the indirect taxes of the country of destination. (The
opposite is called the "origin principle.") The basic notion was that
the introduction or increase of an indirect tax on a good would raise
the price of that good because the producer, who technically had to pay
the tax, would pass it on to the purchaser. It was felt—for balance of
payments reasons as well as domestic employment considerations—
that an exporting industry should not lose its market as a result of
the domestic tax rise. With regard to imports, the justification of
border adjustments was twofold. First, exactly the same reasoning
as applied to export industries also prevailed here: domestic industries
should not be damaged by the influx of foreign goods, which were now
relatively less expensive. In addition, it was felt that the consumer
should not be able to evade the tax by purchasing imported products.*

---

*This paragraph deals only vaguely with the justification origi-
nally given for border tax adjustments because historically they were

Considerations of this kind were peculiar to indirect taxation. Direct taxes, it was felt, did not much raise the prices of products. These taxes were regarded as a burden on the taxed individual or corporation which could not be evaded by purchasing goods from abroad. Therefore, no country pondered border adjustments when it introduced or raised income taxes.

Confirmation by International Law

Many bilateral and multilateral agreements could be cited by which countries affirmed each other's right to subject imported goods to indirect taxation while exempting exports.[11] The most important of these is the General Agreement on Tariffs and Trade (GATT) of 1947.* With regard to border tax adjustments, the framers of GATT did not want to go further than to confirm the basic legality of the existing international practice, leaving technicalities aside.

Uncertainty and Vacillation: The Scope of the Border Adjustments

Until a few years ago, almost all countries with indirect taxes levied them in one of two forms—as a cumulative multi-stage turn-over tax (most Continental European countries) or as a single-stage tax on the wholesale level (Great Britain) or retail level (United States). The single-stage tax automatically implements the destination principle. The multi-stage tax complicates the matter considerably. The number of stages of production varies from good to good and from firm to firm, and correspondingly the tax burden varies on each domestically produced good. If the same burden is to be imposed on imported goods or eliminated in the case of exports, the art of esti-mating becomes crucial. The uncertainties of estimation naturally encourage controversy. Importers argue that the border taxes imposed on imported goods are too high, and domestic producers competing with imports argue that they are too low; exporters argue that the tax rebates on exported products are too low; and competitor nations, as

---

introduced for a variety of vague notions and were not based on thorough scientific deliberations. The example of trading partners applying these adjustments may sometimes have been the decisive factor.

*The tax law of GATT is reproduced in the Appendix.

trading partners, argue that all adjustments, import taxes as well as rebates, are too high. It was generally the third pressure group, the international trading community, that proved to be the strongest, and border adjustments under the cumulative turnover tax were long kept rather low. For example, West Germany, which levied a cumulative turnover tax of 4 percent during the 1950s, for a decade taxed imports only at 4 percent and rebated 3 percent to exporters, which would have meant full equalization only under the unrealistic assumption of enormous vertical integration of all industries. Beginning in 1961, however, the border adjustments were gradually increased in order to subject imported goods to the full turnover tax burden that domestic products had to bear and to relieve exports from their whole tax burden.[12] Certain domestic groups had begun to exert more pressure on the government than foreign countries because the upward revaluation of the German currency in 1961 exposed German industry to increased foreign competition. The fact that five months after the revaluation the border tax adjustments were raised leads to two observations which will reappear in subsequent chapters: (1) there is a relationship between currency exchange rates and border tax adjustments, and (2) these adjustments appear to act as a "protectionist" device.

By 1967, when Germany finally repealed the old turnover tax law, the border adjustments had almost, but apparently not quite, reached the level of "full compensation," which all countries have regarded as their right to achieve and which appears to be sanctioned by GATT. The remaining difference between the domestic rate and the border rate was eliminated by the new value-added tax (VAT). This was one of the reasons for the outcry it provoked in the international trading community.

THE CULPRIT OF THE TAX DISPUTE: THE VALUE-ADDED TAX

The present tax dispute did not begin until after the advent of the VAT as the Common Market's new tax system.[13] This may be surprising, as the VAT is only one further step in a series of developments starting in World War I. But the VAT marks a psychological breaking point for Europe's trading partners. For decades, they had grumblingly accepted the adjustments for the turnover tax, but now they felt that trade was seriously threatened. This was due mainly to the following three changes:

1. With the changeover from the old cumulative turnover tax to the VAT, the rate of the border adjustments increased dramatically (sometimes doubled) simply because of the different mechanism of the tax. Under the old system, a large part of the total tax burden was

due at the wholesale and retail level, i.e., after the importation and after the exportation. The VAT shifted the emphasis to the earlier stages in production, where most of the value is added. As these stages are before importation as well as before exportation, the rate of the border adjustments naturally had to increase without changing the relation between the tax burden of domestic, exported, and imported products and, therefore, without changing the price ratio between domestic and imported goods. The apparent change was an optical illusion, but it nevertheless mattered for the American exporter who suddenly saw the whole iceberg instead of only its tip.

2. The optical change was accompanied by two real changes. One was the fact that any "undercompensation" that previously still may have existed under the multi-stage turnover tax now was corrected to full compensation. The VAT makes it possible to determine the exact tax burden on each product regardless of the stages it has gone through, and consequently no estimates of the adjustments are necessary.

3. Another change, and the most important of all, was the further increase of indirect taxation which so often followed in the wake of a country's first introduction of the VAT. This phenomenon will be discussed in the sections that follow.

Inasmuch as the VAT was the trigger for the present tax dispute and in that it further aggravated the previously existing cleavage between the tax treatment of internationally traded goods on different sides of the Atlantic, it is again important to realize that, like indirect taxation itself, the VAT was not a shrewd protectionist invention but the result of a slow and in itself logical development of the tax systems of many European countries. The next sections of this chapter are therefore devoted to the task of explaining the rise of the VAT. It will be seen that the regulating and shaping forces of the law—domestic and international—and of legal institutions played an important role in this evolution.

BREAKDOWN OF THE CUMULATIVE TURNOVER TAX AND RISE OF THE VALUE-ADDED TAX: THE EXAMPLE OF WEST GERMANY

A Changed Political Scene

The major deficiency of the cumulative turnover tax has already been mentioned: it treats goods differently according to the number of production and distribution stages utilized in producing and marketing the finished product. Complaints had not been scarce, to be sure, but nobody was able to exert the amount of pressure on the German

Parliament necessary to bring about a complete reform of the tax system. It is remarkable that, exactly 50 years after the first introduction of the turnover tax, this pressure finally was supplied by two newly created but powerful courts, the West German Federal Constitutional Court and the EEC Court of Justice. It was not, or at least not in the first place, a change in the law which led to the breakdown of the turnover tax, but a change in society's and the courts' attitude toward the law, reflecting the different political scene in Germany after the establishment of the Federal Republic and in Europe after the creation of the Common Market. The courts that issued the judgments now to be discussed were themselves created as a result of these political changes.*

Border Adjustments and the EEC Court of Justice

Before the Common Market was established, the member states already had adopted the GATT rules on border tax adjustments. They were repeated almost literally in the Rome Treaty (Articles 95 and 96). It was, therefore, not a change in the letter of the law but the new significance that the law gained which brought about the developments leading to the VAT. It seemed clear that no individual businessman could derive rights from the GATT tax rules, but whether the same was true under the EEC law remained a highly controversial issue until the EEC Court of Justice finally decided the question. In June 1966 the court ruled that Article 95 of the Rome Treaty was "self-executing."[14] Immediately after this decision, German importers began to file objections to the import tax assessments they received. It has already been explained that under the cumulative turnover tax system the tax burden on domestic goods can only be estimated. Many German importers now charged that the tax levied on imports was higher than that on like domestic goods and thus in violation of the treaty. Three months after the Court's judgment German customs offices had received 150,000 objections, and each month tens of thousands were added.[15] Through the end of 1967, no less than 330,000 objections had been filed and 25,000 law suits brought in the fiscal courts.[16] The result was, of course, disastrous. Customs offices and fiscal courts were paralyzed to an unprecedented extent. Some courts ordered a stay of the execution of the import tax

---

*The West German Federal Constitutional Court was established in 1951; the EEC Court of Justice was created by the 1957 Rome Treaty.

assessments, causing severe revenue gaps. The traditional border adjustment system had broken down. The German Ministry of Finance had long before prepared a draft of a VAT statute, and acceleration of the turnover tax reform seemed to provide the only solution to the new problem, because—as we have seen—under a VAT the border adjustments exactly match the domestic taxes, and thus such disputes as to the correct rate of the adjustments could not arise.

Competitive Neutrality and the West German
Federal Constitutional Court

The major deficiency of the traditional turnover tax, the cumulative effect, not only makes "correct" border adjustments impossible but also works in favor of vertically integrated firms. This discrimination between different firms and industries is not a deliberate one but is simply a side-effect of the tax system. It is not a necessary side-effect, however, as the example of the VAT clearly shows. (The VAT had been known in theory since World War I and in practice— applied by France—since 1937.) For this reason, the compatibility of a cumulative turnover tax with the equal protection clause of the German Constitution had been a troublesome question for decades. It may be noted that the earlier Constitution of 1919 had contained an equal protection clause[17] and that it was taken over into the Constitution of 1949.[18] The issue was temporarily resolved in 1934 when the Minister of Finance was empowered to take any measures that would equalize the tax burdens of vertically integrated firms and non-integrated firms. This broad yielding of power to the executive reflects the totalitarian views then prevailing and was struck down by the newly created Federal Constitutional Court in 1958 as violative of the rules of the 1949 Constitution dealing with the separation of powers.[19] Immediately thereafter, the Ministry of Finance began to tackle the problem of a complete reform of the turnover tax. As early as 1960, the first draft of a VAT statute was published. In 1966, the question of compatibility with the equal protection clause finally came before the Constitutional Court. It decided that the cumulative turnover tax statute lacked competitive neutrality and that, therefore, the time of its validity had to be limited.[20] Noting that since its 1958 decision eight years had passed, the court nevertheless acknowledged the enormous complexity of such a reform and conceded that the time for the legislature to act had not yet run out. A definite time limit was not set, but the threat that the court would finally declare the turnover tax law unconstitutional was clear; in view of the complete dependence of the German budget on the turnover tax, this was a formidable threat indeed.* By mere coincidence, this decision was handed down six months after the disastrous decision of the EEC Court of Justice which was discussed above. Even more than the latter judgment, it accelerated the reform of the old turnover tax law greatly. The German Parliament, faced with these two decisions, had no choice. Only five months later, in May of 1967, the new VAT statute was passed. It took effect on January 1, 1968.

THE PROLIFERATION OF THE VAT IN
RECENT YEARS

Tax Harmonization in the EEC

The Unresolved Tax Dispute in the European
Coal and Steel Community

When the European Coal and Steel Community (ECSC), the limited but important forerunner of the EEC, was established in 1952, the tax systems of all its member states were characterized by heavy reliance on turnover taxes, but among themselves they nevertheless differed greatly. The French and the German systems especially showed little resemblance: Germany levied a comparatively low turnover tax and applied "undercompensation" at the borders, whereas France relied on a very high VAT with the full border adjustments that are typical for this tax. Thus, Germany found herself at odds with France in a

---

*This instance of pressure exerted by the Constitutional Court on the legislature is not unique. In 1969, for example, the Court declared that Parliament could no longer retard the reform of the law affecting illegitimate children, a reform prescribed by the Constitutions of 1919 and 1949. A definite time limit for the validity of the old law was set by the court: the next general election, which was to be held eight months later (Judgment of January 29, 1969, 25 BVerfG 167). The reform statute was passed in time. Had Parliament not managed to meet the deadline—given the controversial views on the subject that would not have been surprising—the courts would have had to create a new law for illegitimate children on their own, i.e., case law would have taken the place of the by then unconstitutional old statute. This shows that the Constitutional Court is not timid in carrying out a threat of this kind, even if the social consequences might be serious.

position quite similar to that of the United States vis-à-vis the EEC today. German producers had always resented the high French border adjustments, and they tried to use the ECSC as a vehicle to pursue their interests, pointing out that in a partial common market such "competitive distortions" should not be allowed. In 1953, a committee of economic experts was appointed by the High Authority of the ECSC to resolve the question. It concluded that the ECSC members should continue to apply the destination principle to their trade in coal and steel and that this would not distort competitive conditions, whereas the origin principle would lead to distortions unless it was applied to all other goods as well.[21]

Despite the authority of the committee's chairman, Ian Tinbergen, the report was acidly criticized by many economists who charged that the committee was not familiar with the basic economic theories of tax shifting. (The merits of the report will be discussed in Chapter 3.) German businessmen therefore were encouraged to continue their complaints. With the establishment of the EEC in 1958, the dispute became aggravated.

The Choice of the VAT as the Common EEC System

The unresolved ECSC tax dispute, the uncertainty of the level of border adjustments under the cumulative turnover tax, the latter's lack of competitive neutrality, and finally the wish to abolish all special tax treatment of border-crossing trade within the EEC led to the proposal of a basic harmonization of the turnover tax systems in the member states, which was put forth by the EEC Commission in 1962. The five members using a cumulative turnover tax were to adopt the VAT, and France was to align her VAT to the new system.[22] In 1967 the proposal was finally adopted by the Council which directed the member states to effectuate these changes by 1970.[23]

Resistance and Compliance

The first countries to comply with the directive were the old foes in the ECSC tax dispute. As of January 1, 1968, France extended her VAT to the retail sector, and Germany introduced a 10 percent VAT. The reasons for Germany's quick compliance have already been indicated.* The other countries had greater difficulties in

---

*Commonly, the harmonization efforts in the EEC toward a common VAT system are cited as the major reason for Germany's adoption of the VAT. It is submitted here that other forces, already

reforming their turnover tax systems. The EEC Council had to alter
the original 1970 deadline for the harmonization because Belgium and
Italy were not able to meet it (the present deadline is 1973). Belgium's
VAT went into effect in 1971, but Italy still has not passed the new
law. The main difficulty in Italy has been the inclusion of the retail
sector. Italian retailers are unfamiliar with the complicated kind of
bookkeeping the VAT requires, and their tax morale is low.

The VAT in the EEC Today

In order to achieve some kind of a progression mitigating the
regressive effect of an indirect tax, all countries apply several rates—
usually a normal, a reduced, and a high rate.* The reduced rate is
mainly for food, the high rate for several luxuries. The normal rates
are presently as follows: Belgium 20 percent, France 23 percent,
West Germany 11 percent, Luxembourg 8 percent, The Netherlands
14 percent. Italy contemplates 15 percent.**

----

visible before the first Harmonization Directive of April 1967, all but
compelled Parliament to reform the turnover tax law. The harmonization efforts, partly induced by the same forces, would not even have
been necessary in this respect. See previous discussion of "The
Breakdown of the Cumulative Turnover Tax Rise of the Value-
added Tax: The Example of West Germany."

*These rates are applied to prices exclusive of tax. Some coun-
tries express their rates as a percentage of the gross sales price
(inclusive VAT). The difference can, of course, be considerable and
must always be taken into account when VAT rates of various countries
are compared. Since 1970, France applies, like the other EEC countries, the first of the two methods.

**It is planned that in the future all member states will apply
about the same rate. (The final turnover tax system of the EEC will
be discussed later, in Part II.) Therefore, Germany, Luxembourg,
and the Netherlands will certainly increase their rates and the other
countries might lower them, so that finally they will meet somewhere
in the middle. This is one of the reasons why the VAT has the tendency
to increase at least in certain countries. The Netherlands raised the
normal rate from 12 percent to 14 percent in 1971; Germany is contemplating an increase from the present 11 percent to 12 percent or
more. Needless to say, such steps are hotly debated political affairs,
and therefore all changes will be slow.

The VAT in the New EEC Member States

The United Kingdom, which is almost certain to join the EEC, announced in 1972 that introduction of a VAT at 10 percent is planned. The Irish Minister of Finance made such an announcement as early as 1970. The prospective Scandinavian EEC members already apply VAT systems: Denmark with 12.5 percent, Norway with 20 percent.

The Spread of the VAT to Countries Outside the Common Market

Any statement on the geographical extension of the VAT is likely to become obsolete within a short time because changeovers to the VAT are frequent and have become a familiar picture in recent years. The VAT has proved to be a contagious tax system.

The two European Associates of the EEC, Greece and Turkey, have limited VAT systems. Those Western European countries which for reasons of political neutrality are neither EEC members nor candidates for membership also favor the new tax: Sweden applies a VAT at 17 percent, and Austria plans introduction of the VAT in 1973.[24]

Outside Europe, the VAT has taken root in Latin America: Brazil and Uruguay have adopted it; Argentina, Mexico, and most recently Chile published draft statutes.*

The main reason for these changes is the realization of the advantages the VAT has over the cumulative turnover tax.[25] But especially in Europe, there are two additional reasons. One is that most countries in Western Europe expect to become members or associates of the Common Market. As the developments in the ECSC and EEC proved, a harmonization of indirect taxation becomes increasingly desirable with the intensifying of economic integration. The other reason, and the most interesting for this study, is that substitution of a VAT for a cumulative turnover tax and even more for a direct tax is generally believed to improve a country's balance

---

*To date, the realm of the VAT seems to be limited to Western Europe and Latin America. Japan contemplated it in 1949 on the advice of the United States and in particular of tax expert Carl S. Shoup of New York. But the proposal was rejected—reportedly because businessmen feared that they could not shift the tax forward to the consumer. The VAT was the only measure proposed by the Shoup Mission that has never been put into effect.

of trade.* One country's surplus is the other's deficit, and so the introduction of the VAT in one country may well provoke the same action in another as a kind of retaliation or re-establishment of the previous competitive situation. Objectionable as it may be to change the domestic tax structure for balance of payments considerations, it is beyond doubt that this thought loomed large in the minds of legislators—especially where, as in Norway in 1969, not only the old turnover tax but also a part of the country's direct tax was replaced by a VAT.

---

*This belief is justified when a VAT is substituted for a turnover tax without a change in the total revenue provided that border compensation under the turnover tax was not adequate ("undercompensation"). Whether it is justified in other cases is a problem that will be taken up in Part II. In any event, the belief is widely shared, and this provides another explanation for the fact that many countries, once converted to the VAT, tend to increase it at the expense of other f of taxation.

THE BACKGROUND: THE DEFICIT IN
THE UNITED STATES BALANCE OF PAYMENTS

The importance American policy-makers attribute to the border tax dispute must be seen in the context of the balance of payments problem that has plagued the United States for well over a decade.[1] Many attempts have been made to reduce the outflow of dollars from this country as well as to induce a greater influx of foreign currency. It is not necessary here to discuss the merits of these efforts. Despite the fact that some well-known economists have urged a "passive" balance of payments policy for the United States, the official position is still one of great concern about the chronic deficit. A strong trade surplus is regarded as the major means of countervailing the outflow of money resulting from foreign aid, military expenditures, and private investment abroad.

The United States has always enjoyed a trade surplus vis-à-vis the EEC;[2] however, that does not mean that this surplus could not be increased. A change in the adjustment practice might have the desired effect,* and the United States is therefore very interested in bringing

---

*However, it would not necessarily have this effect. The impact of an abolition of European border tax adjustments on the United States trade balance would depend upon the domestic economic situation in the United States. If unemployment were high, the trade balance would be improve. But if the economy were already using all available labor resources, the immediate effect on exports and imports would in the longer run be countervailed by the consequent overheating of the American economy.

about such a change. Most businessmen, economists, and lawyers would, of course, raise their objections to the present border tax adjustments regardless of the U.S. balance of payments. But the fact that vital American interests are at stake has certainly provoked considerable academic and even public interest in the subject.

THE CHALLENGE: UNITED STATES ARGUMENTS AGAINST THE PRESENT BORDER TAX ADJUSTMENTS

An Attempt to Classify the Arguments

Objections to the present border tax adjustment practice have been numerous. Experts and nonexperts alike have stated their views, impartial scholars as well as spokesmen for particular interests.* This debate, in which so many different voices can be heard, is passionate, and it forms the vivid background for the discussion of the problem that follows in Part II. As the reader may expect that, in the course of this discussion, the various issues will be evaluated and clarified and that he will be equipped with answers to all possible questions on the subject, an attempt is made to familiarize him at the outset with the colorful gamut of objections that have been raised against the customary border tax adjustments.

In trying to disentangle the various arguments, one can discern four different styles of argumentation, distinguished by the point of view taken: that of a businessman, that of an economic expert, that of a lawyer, and finally that of a professional policy-maker. It is not submitted, of course, that only economists have investigated the problems of economic theory here involved, or that the discussion of the legal issues has been limited to lawyers. Indeed, the very fact that many lawyers have dealt with the problem in economic terms has contributed to the enormous confusion of the debate and has obscured the real issues.[3]

---

*The presentation of the arguments against border adjustments that follows is not merely a series of excerpts from such writings. In many instances, the advocatus diaboli position is taken and there is an attempt to invent, extend, or support all possible objections to the adjustments. The purpose of this exercise is to develop the whole spectrum of questions that must be answered in the following chapters.

The Businessman's View: Unfairness

A Comparison of Costs

When European exports receive a rebate of about 15 percent
while American exports get none, and imports into Europe are subjected to a 15 percent import tax while imports into the United States
pass the border tax-free, it seems rather obvious that Americans
are at a disadvantage—in their own market as well as in the European
market or in third countries. In this simple form the argument is
often expressed by American leaders when they publicly refer to the
problem, e.g., by former President Lyndon B. Johnson in his 1968
Statement on the Balance of Payments,[4] or by the former Secretary
of Commerce, Maurice Stans, on numerous occasions.[5] It is not a very
profound argument, but without doubt it reflects the feeling of the
American businessman.

J. Frank Gaston and William J. J. Smith, authors of a recent
American study, are of the same persuasion but try to offer a better
foundation for the argument. They made a thorough empirical investigation of the operation of border tax adjustments,[6] and their results
may be summed up as follows. For shipments from the United States,
landed prices in a European port range from 104 percent to 176 percent
of the price at the U.S. shipping port. On the reverse journey across
the Atlantic, the range is from 88 percent to 134 percent of the
European price at the shipping port.[7] The "cost of entry," which is
indicated by these figures, consists mainly of freight, insurance,
customs duties, and compensatory taxes. Especially in the case of
France, the last outweighs all the other items. It can be seen that
the "cost of entry" is not reciprocal. For European goods, it might
even be negative, i.e., the products are actually less expensive in the
United States than in Europe, despite freight, insurance, and tariff.*

Gaston and Smith take pains to prove that the entry costs are
not reciprocal, but they fail to say what the conclusion from that fact
should be—in an economic or legal or perhaps even moral sense. The
reader is simply left with the vague impression that something "unfair" is going on.

---

*Similar observations are made with respect to shipment from
the United States and EEC to a common destination. The "cost of entry"
into the third market is lower for EEC competitors. Even if a firm
in the EEC charges a higher domestic price than the competing U.S.
firm, this apparent disadvantage can be overcome and the Europeans
might undersell the Americans in the third country.

In more general terms, the argument goes on to say that the higher the VAT is in a foreign country, the more difficult it will be for the United States to compete with that country. It is even conceivable that a country might increase its VAT to such a degree that no firm in the United States could compete with its producers. This gloomy outlook ends the first complaint of the businessman. He offers, however, another argument, which is more sophisticated.

Are Taxes Production Costs?

The exemption of an exported good from indirect taxation seems to amount to an export subsidy because tax revenues are spent by the government partly on projects that reduce business costs. The more services, such as subsidized national transportation systems, industry research grants, public police and fire protection, postal services, etc., the government provides, the more will the production cost of a certain good be reduced for the businessman. The core of the argument is this: The higher the taxes in a country are, the less expensive will a product of this country be if it is freed from all taxes. It is possible, therefore, to regard taxes, at least partly, as production costs: the producer pays money to the government and receives cost-reducing services in return. It seems unjustified, therefore, to rebate the tax when the product is exported.[8] If exports were freed from all taxes, exporting producers in countries with high taxes would have an advantage over those in low-tax countries. Border tax adjustments are attempts to create artificially an effect as if all countries applied the same indirect tax rates, i.e., they adjust for differences on the revenue side, without taking account of the resulting differences in cost-reducing government expenditures.

Although the argument appears to be convincing, almost irrefutable, one flaw in it is easily recognizable. It is impossible to say by how much business costs are reduced as a result of government services, and in any event only a very small part of the tax revenue is spent on such services. However, the argument can be refined even further in order to counter that attack. In determining whether tax revenue in effect helps to lower the production costs of a product, not only government services to producers but also those to consumers must be considered. If a comparatively socialized country offers inexpensive housing, free health care, and artificially low food prices, it may thereby weaken the demands for higher wages that would otherwise occur, and so help to keep labor costs low.* Thus, a large

---

*Other expenditures, such as free public education, can be viewed from both angles: they reduce the cost of living, and (in promoting skilled workers and scientists, for example) they directly help to reduce production costs.

part of the total tax revenue is spent in a way that in effect reduces
production costs.*

The Economist's View: Disregard of Modern
Economic Theory

The Theory of Tax Shifting

The criticism of economic experts is directed mainly against
the alleged disregard of modern understanding of tax shifting. The
present border tax adjustment practice, they say, rests upon the
assumption that direct taxes do not influence prices whereas indirect
taxes are shifted forward to the consumer**—hence the adjustments
are made for indirect taxes only. This assumption seems to be justified by classical economic theory,*** but it has never been unchallenged, and today a wealth of theoretical as well as empirical studies
can be cited to refute it.[9] Most critics agree on one point: if the

---

*In developing this thought further, one could introduce a con-
cept of "net incidence" of taxes on industries—the amount of taxes
paid for which business gets nothing in return. Only that amount
should be rebated to exporters.

**Whether the border adjustment practice really rests on this
assumption is, of course, difficult to ascertain. It may be correct when
the question is asked in historical terms (see Chapter 1). However,
when the rationale of the border tax adjustments, especially of the
GATT tax law, is to be ascertained without reference to the origin of
the practice, justifications independent of any shifting assumptions may
be found. This will be discussed extensively in Part II. What these
critics really mean, however, is another thing—namely, that the present border tax adjustments can only be justified when the traditional
shifting assumptions are made, and that otherwise they create distortions.

***The view that prices are not affected by the imposition of a
profit tax is supported by economic theory not only—as is often alleged—
for a situation of competition, but also for the case of a monopoly.
In the first case, different firms may earn different profits, but as
the "marginal" firm earns no profit at all, a profit tax cannot lead to
a higher price: the marginal firm, which would not have to raise its
price, would otherwise undersell its competitors. In the second case,
the price is determined by the intersection of the marginal cost and
marginal revenue curves, i.e., by the monopolist's search for maximum

traditional shifting assumptions were true, the present border tax adjustments would be unobjectionable—they would be "trade-neutral" and neither "distorting" nor "protectionist." But classical economic theory does not mirror today's actual business practice, and the adjustments <u>are</u> "protectionist," "distorting," and not "neutral." Essentially three reasons are given for this view; the following discussion deals with each in turn.

Full Border Tax Adjustments: Export Subsidies and Import Restrictions ?

A simplified numerical example may show how border adjustments work when the indirect tax is not entirely shifted forward into the price. Assume that a certain product passes from firm A to firm B, from B to C, and from C to the exporter, D. A, B, and C each have factor costs of 40 and a profit of 10, so that each of them adds 50 to the value of the product. Accordingly, D buys it for 150. If now a 10 percent VAT is imposed and each firm shifts it fully into the price it charges for the product, D will pay 165 to C. As A, B, and C each paid 5 to the government, 15 will be rebated to D. It is easy to see that D's ability to compete in the export market is entirely unchanged. If, however, the competitive situation makes it impossible for A, B, and C to shift more than three fifths of the tax into the price, and there is no way of changing the costs, they will reduce their profits from 10 to about 8. A sells to B for 53 (instead of 55 as in the previous case), B to C for 106, and C to D for 159. Again, however, A, B, and C each paid (almost) 5 to the government, so that 15 are rebated to D. It is now possible for D to lower the price he charges (or to make a larger profit). He receives an "export subsidy" of about 6.*

A corresponding example could, of course, be presented to show that in this case an importer's competitive situation in the domestic market would be worsened because after the introduction of the tax he would have to pay 15 to the government on each imported good whereas the price of comparable domestic products would have risen only by 9.

---

profits. A profit tax will leave the price unaffected because any increase in the price would decrease profits before tax and therefore decrease profits after tax.

*In this case of only partial forward shifting, the exact numbers are 8.18 instead of "8," 4.82 instead of "5," and 5.46 instead of "6."

It is well known that export subsidies as well as impediments to imports partly destroy the benefits of free trade (discussed in Chapter 3), and consequently many writers quickly concluded that the same must be true of the present border tax adjustments.[10] The opinion that a reduction of factor costs or profits that is induced by a tax may constitute an export subsidy has even led to the logical although somewhat surprising conclusion that in the case of a retail sales tax that is not fully shifted forward a special export tax is required to offset the competitive export advantage gained from a drop in net producer prices.[11] The policy proposal resulting from this opinion is the following: border adjustments should reflect the actual degree of tax shifting.[12]

The Tax Structure Argument

"Competitive Distortions." Most economists who critize the present adjustment practice have focused on the discrimination between in-direct and direct taxes. To allow border adjustments only for the former but not for the latter is, they say, arbitrary—because both kinds of tax are at least partly reflected in prices—and favors "indirect tax countries" over "direct tax countries." Eminent writers in the United States (Richard A. Musgrave) as well as in the EEC (Günter Schmölders) have taken this view; to avoid partiality, a study of Hans Gerber, a Swiss tax expert, is presented here to familiarize the reader with the typical argument. Gerber presents the following example:[13] Producers in countries A and B have exactly the same production costs before taxes, say 100 (dollars or any other monetary unit, as computed from the respective local currency at the official exchange rate). The total tax burden is, in both countries, 32 percent of this net price and the producers are able to shift all taxes fully forward, so that the gross price of the product is 132 in both coun-tries.* It is now assumed that A has a VAT of 20 percent and B one of 10 percent, the remainder of the tax being provided by income taxation. As there are border adjustments only for the VAT and not for the direct tax, A's product will cost 121 in B, whereas B's product

---

*The simplified model behind these numbers is this: If total taxation in a country is 32 percent of the GNP, 32 percent out of the price paid for the "average" consumption or investment good (or service) will end up in that country's treasury, whether by means of indirect taxation or income taxes. It is this "average" good which Gerber has in mind.

costs 144 in A (the combined rebates and import taxes of 10 percent
and 20 percent, respectively, lead to this result).* That means that
A will undersell B,** despite identical production costs and tax burdens.
Gerber concludes that the border tax adjustments create "distortions."
He further says that these distortions will differ from industry to
industry and cannot, therefore, be remedied by the exchange rate.

The term "distortion of competition" is often used in this context;[14] others prefer to speak of a "trade protection advantage."[15]
Although the meaning of these words is usually not explained, some
authors have expressed their concern in more specific terms and
have pointed out that under the present system goods exported from
a "direct tax country" to an "indirect tax country" are subject to
double taxation, whereas goods traveling in the reverse direction
evade the tax altogether.[16] The words "double taxation" and "tax
evasion" are considered to be persuasive per se.

Proposed Solutions. The opinion that the present border adjustments
create distortions in the trade between countries with different tax
structures, i.e., different reliance on indirect taxes, has led to two
proposals. The first is the abolition of the traditional border tax
adjustments and the adoption of the origin principle. This has been
advocated, e.g., by Schmölders, who regards all taxes as "location
costs", exactly like wages, prices of raw materials, etc.[17] There is
a very convincing thought in that argument. Why, Schmölders asks,
should the individual manufacturer artificially be taken out of the
general economic context of his country with regard to taxes, when
innumerable other domestic factors (economic policy, wage level,
antitrust law, factor-endowment, investment, technology, etc.), for
which there is no border adjustment, all work together to determine
his price?

The other proposal, which seems to have more support, calls
for extension of the border adjustments to direct taxes.[18] The two

---

*A's product costs 132 within A (110 + 20 percent VAT). It gets
a rebate of 22 if it is exported, and consequently the importer in B
buys it for 110. B levies 10 percent import tax, so that the price in
B is 121.

**This is, of course, the same as the argument already raised
by the businessman, with the difference that we deal now with it in a
theoretical way and draw economic conclusions. Similar numerical
examples have been supplied by many writers, including, for example,
Günter Schmölders.

major treatises on GATT law cautiously consider this to be, at least
theoretically, the most sensible view.[19] However, it is not entirely
clear whether the authors have in mind a uniform rate of adjustments
or whether they would prefer to rebate for each exported product the
amount of direct or indirect taxes that has been shifted into the price
of that particular product, and impose similar import taxes. It will
be shown in Part II how important this distinction is. It seems that
both authors point to the second possibility: Kenneth W. Dam speaks
of a "case-by-case approach to the border tax adjustment problem";
John H. Jackson wants to "neutralize the domestic tax burden effect
on competition." Inasmuch as competition is primarily a micro-economic
phenomenon—different products are competing in the world market,
not different countries—such a neutralization could be brought about only
by differentiated treatment of different products.

The Consumer Benefit Doctrine

One justification for the present border adjustments, it is said,
is the following: As the indirect tax is assumed to be shifted forward
and borne by the consumer, the latter ought to get something in return
for his tax: the benefit of government services.[20] Therefore, a foreign
consumer must be exempted from the tax. On the other hand, a
domestic consumer shall not be able to avoid the tax by purchasing
imported goods and to get the services of his government anyway—
therefore the imposition of an import tax. This justification apparently
rests on the traditional shifting assumption and seems to be shaken,
together with that assumption itself, by more modern insights.

The Lawyer's View: Violation of GATT

Indirect Taxes and GATT

The GATT rules on border tax adjustments do not use such
precise technical terms as "turnover tax" or even such vague ones as
"indirect tax."[21] Instead, adjustments are allowed for domestic taxes
"applied to products" (Article III 2), "imposed in respect of products"
(Article II), and "borne by products" (Article VI). In view of such
obscurity it is, of course, not too difficult for a lawyer to challenge
the identification of a particular tax (e.g., the VAT) with the tax sup-
posedly meant by GATT. Two different ways of arguing are conceivable.
First, one could take a rather formal view and maintain that the
VAT is not a tax "on products" (as a retail sales tax would clearly
be) but a species closely akin to the income tax, using the earnings of
the firm as a sort of income calculation.[22]

Second, the new studies on tax shifting could be used to point out that only that part of the VAT which is actually shifted forward into the price is "borne by the product," and that, accordingly, the border adjustments must be smaller than the domestic tax rate if full shifting cannot be assumed. If it could be established that border adjustments that exceed the rate of the shifting in fact lead to severe economic distortions (Part II will deal with this question), the Preamble of GATT, containing the Contracting Parties' pledge to avoid such distortions,* would, it seems, mandate this construction of the GATT tax law.** The lawyer is familiar with instances where the meaning of a certain legal rule was held to have changed with time, where new social developments or—as in this case—new scientific insights led to a different interpretation of the law. The fact that these new developments were not known to the historical legislator (in this case to the "Contracting Parties" in 1947) and may not have been anticipated at that time is irrelevant (see Chapter 6).

Direct Taxes and GATT

When the view is accepted that income taxes as well as indirect taxes are reflected in prices, it can be argued that income taxes should, at least partly, be considered to be "borne by products." The proper test to decide whether border adjustments are allowed by GATT would be the price effect of the tax. This interpretation of the law has been proposed by Richard A. Musgrave, a leading economist.[23]

The Government Representative's View: Changed Circumstances

Government officials who are in charge of international economic negotiations sometimes try to read something like a <u>clausula rebus</u>

---

*"Recognizing that their relations . . . should be conducted with a view to . . . developing the full use of the resources of the world and expanding the production and exchange of goods . . . being desirous of contributing to these objectives by entering into . . . arrangements directed . . . to the elimination of discriminatory treatment in international commerce."

**However, none of the authors who consider the present adjustments to be distorting because they exceed the actual rate of shifting seems to have taken this view, nor has it been expressed by other writers.

sic stantibus into GATT. In a technical legal sense this would mean
that GATT rules should be applied only as long as the basic circumstances upon which they were built remain valid.* But the government
negotiator's invocation of the clausula does not go that far. He uses
it for a psychological purpose: to clear the ground for a reconsidera-
tion of the old rules. Two circumstances, it is said, have changed
drastically since 1947 and therefore the border tax rules must now
be scrutinized and perhaps changed. First, in 1947 the United States
enjoyed a $10 billion trade surplus. The border tax rules, which
favored the European countries, were thought by U.S. negotiators to
be a good way to ease the dollar shortage. Today, this justification
for the yielding attitude of the United States no longer exists. Second,
25 years ago tariffs and quotas were the major obstacle to trade, and
little attention was paid to relatively minor issues such as border tax
adjustments. But over the decades tariffs came down and quotas were
eliminated, and thus the other trade barriers became more prominent
and important. Therefore, these nontariff barriers (and especially
the border tax adjustments) must now be evaluated in the light of
their new relative importance.**

THE THREAT OF ACTION: THE UNITED
STATES ARSENAL OF TRADE WEAPONS

Multilateral Action

The potential significance of the tax dispute between the EEC and
the United States is indicated by the amount of trade between the two
protagonists ($12.8 billion in 1969) and the average rate of the border
tax adjustments (about 15 percent, considerably higher than the average
tariff rate of the United States as well as the EEC). However, little
has happened yet on the international scene. There were, however,
official charges and defenses,[24] and since 1968 a GATT Working
Party, established at the request of the United States, has been

----

*The clausula r.s.s. is of considerable importance in the field
of public international law, but its applicability to GATT has not been
suggested seriously.

**This statement, which can be heard frequently and which, on
its face, seems to be so true, is in fact very misleading with respect
to border tax adjustments; this will be explained in Chapter 4.

discussing the problem.* Any significant multilateral action has
apparently been barred by the EEC.** The United States has not yet
utilized the GATT complaint procedures (Article XXIII: Nullification
or Impairment and Article XXVIII: Modification of Schedules), apparently because it seems very doubtful whether GATT has been
violated at all by the EEC countries. If there is no such violation,
the only recourse seems to be an international agreement on new
rules, and this is impossible without the cooperation of the EEC.
Attention in the United States, therefore, has turned to possible
unilateral action.

Unilateral Action

United States Border Tax Adjustments

It has been proposed that the United States should introduce its
own border adjustments. These could be adjustments either for income taxes—assuming a change in the letter or in the interpretation
of GATT—or for certain federal, state, and local indirect taxes for
which there are not yet adjustments although they would presumably
be permitted by GATT. The latter proposal is embodied in several
recent drafts of a new trade bill. According to Treasury estimates,

---

*Almost nothing is known publicly about these discussions.
The annual supplements to the GATT Documents merely indicate that
the Working Party is still holding meetings in Geneva. Some un-
published interim reports and statements by the Working Party or the
representative of the United States to it were circulated privately.

**From the point of view the United States, it seems that the
Working Party must be regarded as a failure. The VAT is now practically implemented as the uniform EEC turnover tax system, and all
countries apply the full rate to internationally traded goods. There
might have been some chance of working out a "stand-still agreement" before the changeover to the VAT, which would have kept down
the border adjustment rates. But now, after the changeover has
been effected, it seems extremely unlikely that the EEC countries
will reduce the border rates they just increased. The United States
has missed the moment most favorable for its cause. It is not here
submitted, however, that this is due to lack of skill on the side of the
American negotiators. Rather it seems that the adamant resistance
of the EEC defeated all attempts of the United States to reach an agreement.

a drawback computed to cover indirect tax costs included in export prices would average about 2 percent.[25]

United States Export Incentives and Import Duties

The United States has no power under present legislation to provide subsidies on exports to the EEC in order to outweigh the VAT. However, passage of an export-oriented tax proposal already presented to Congress is urged by the U.S. Government. The device under consideration is the "domestic international sales corporation." It will be examined in Part III.

Concerning imports, the U.S. Countervailing Duty Law seems to offer the possibility of imposing special duties on imported goods that benefit from VAT rebates.

Adoption of the VAT in the United States

The U.S. Treasury Department is studying in depth the possibility of introducing the VAT in the United States, partly as a device of improving the country's trade balance. It is being considered whether a VAT should supplant other forms of taxation at federal and state levels.[26] Such a change would encounter much resistance, especially in the Democratic Party (due to the fact that the VAT is considered to be a "regressive" tax). It is impossible to predict which forces will prevail. Apart from all the domestic problems, it has often been questioned whether adoption of a VAT with full border adjustments in the United States for balance of trade reasons would be a sensible approach to international economic policy. This question can only be answered after it has been clarified how, in the sense of an ideal solution, domestic tax laws should deal with internationally traded goods. This is the topic of the following chapters.

THE POLICY ISSUE: HOW SHOULD DOMESTIC TAX LAWS DEAL WITH INTERNATIONALLY TRADED GOODS?

Part II raises the question of an ideal solution to the problem of taxation of internationally traded goods.* After an answer to this question has been formulated in the following three chapters, Part III will compare the current international law of border tax adjustments with the optimal solution.

Before approaching a question of this kind, it is necessary to define the policies to be pursued and the goals to be achieved.[1] Basically, the following policies should be distinguished:

1. A country can introduce those border tax adjustments which most effectively further its national interests. The power of a state to levy taxes, the fiscal power, is not only the financial foundation of all government activity but it is also a very important instrument of national policy, which can be used to serve various social and economic purposes. If a country adopts a purely national viewpoint, it will tend to choose those border tax adjustments which least interfere with its fiscal power.

2. Pressure exerted by their trading partners as well as selfish considerations may induce nations to adopt a cosmopolitan point of view. If a country's border tax adjustments reduce the economic welfare of the trading community as a whole, it is likely not only that they will interfere directly with the welfare of the country adopting such policies (e.g., by diminishing the potential advantages to be gained from international trade) but also that they will provoke retaliatory action by other states that may injure the principal country even more. The resulting damage to national welfare may well outweigh the advantages of these border tax adjustments for domestic policy. This may lead a country to institute adjustments that most effectively further the world economy as a whole.

3. One policy is mandated by the taxing country's purely national interests as well as by those of its trading partners: avoidance of disequilibrium in the international balance of payments. Disequilibrium is generally undesirable for various economic reasons, and inasmuch

---

*Only world trade in goods is considered. Taxation of internationally traded services (shipping, insurance, tourism) encounters numerous difficult practical problems that do not arise in the case of goods. Treatment of these practical problems is omitted here.

as one country's surplus means another's deficit, national and international interests are here intertwined. Pursuing this policy, a country will apply border tax adjustments in a way that makes its balance of payments independent of domestic tax changes.

Obviously, a country will only be able to achieve its economic goals—such as maximum efficiency, growth, full employment, price stability—if it manages to pursue all of these policies harmoniously. Other goals—such as social control, maximization of revenue—mandate strengthening the national tax power in a way that does not conflict with the interests of foreign countries. Therefore, the "ideal" border tax adjustments are those which are fully acceptable to the community of trading nations as a whole and which simultaneously do not impair the fiscal power of the taxing country.

These considerations will set the course of the following investigation. At the outset, the compatibility of border tax adjustments with maximum efficiency of the world economy is considered. A cosmopolitan point of view is taken, in that it is especially in the field of efficiency that one country's achievements can be impaired by its trading partners' defaults and retaliations. Later, the investigation will turn to the balance of payments problem. Finally, the relationship between border tax adjustments and the national fiscal power is considered.

The distinction of the three policies described above is necessarily a crude one in this complex area. The following pages will show that within these broad outlines many different, often conflicting, policies can be pursued. It will be necessary to define these policies, to ponder their importance, and to consider possible means of resolving conflicts.

One example may demonstrate how important it is to distinguish different policies. If it can be shown either that border tax adjustments are necessary to achieve maximum efficiency of the world economy or that they must be abandoned or modified in order to achieve it, the justification or objection, whichever it may be, applies to the total existing adjustments. The conclusions that can be drawn with respect to the goal of balance of payments equilibrium, in contrast, are much more limited. If border tax adjustments are shown either to change the trade balance or to be necessary to protect this balance from disturbing changes, the extent of the resulting justification or objection depends upon the present balance of payments of the countries involved* and upon previous currency exchange rate

---

*For instance, if the border adjustments have helped to equalize a previously existing deficit in the balance of payments, they cannot be challenged.

changes.* In principle, the question whether border adjustments should be terminated, continued, or introduced for balance of payments reasons will be relevant only for future changes in domestic taxation, not for the total existing adjustments, in that the parity changes of the last decade can be assumed to have adjusted for any influence of border tax adjustments on foreign trade.**

---

*For instance, if a country appreciates its currency in order to reduce its trade surplus, the effect of border tax adjustments which were one of the reasons for the original surplus is thereby canceled out. If these border adjustments had not existed, the country would presumably not have appreciated its currency, or at least not to such an extent. Thus, after the appreciation the border tax adjustments can no longer be challenged for balance of payments reasons.

**Almost all of the important trading nations changed the par values of their currencies in December 1971. In addition, the two largest "VAT countries" in the EEC effected several such changes during the last decade: France devalued her currency in 1958 and again in 1969, whereas West Germany appreciated its currency in 1961 and in 1969. Other VAT countries changing the par values of their currencies even before 1971 include the Netherlands (appreciation 1961) and Denmark (devaluation 1967).

3

ECONOMIC EFFECTS
OF BORDER TAX ADJUSTMENTS
ON WORLD PRODUCTION
AND WORLD TRADE

BORDER TAX ADJUSTMENTS AND
ECONOMIC EFFICIENCY

Economic Efficiency

The first part of this chapter is devoted to a study of the
compatibility of different taxes and border tax adjustments with
maximum efficiency of the world economy.[1] The viewpoint is—in
accordance with the considerations discussed in the Introduction to
Part II—a cosmopolitan one: economic welfare is defined as the sum
of the welfare of all world citizens. Maximum efficiency has been
attained when it is impossible to make one person in the world better
off without making another worse off. This means basically two
things. First, productive resources in the world must be used in the
most efficient manner, so that maximum output is achieved. Second,
the goods produced must be distributed to consumers in a way that
gives every individual the greatest possible satisfaction given the
limitation of his income. Thus, the two basic conditions for efficiency
are the "maximization of production" and the "optimization of trade."[2]
In order not to burden the treatment of the tax problems with an
explanation of these conditions, they are considered at the outset.

In the following investigation, it will generally be assumed that
perfect competition prevails in all markets, that free trade is not
interfered with, and that—apart from the taxes under consideration--
no circumstances* exist that might cause economic inefficiency.
These are, of course, entirely unrealistic assumptions. However,

---

*E.g., external economies or diseconomies, governmental
subsidies, market interventions.

they can be justified when the achievement of maximum economic efficiency is acknowledged as the ultimate goal. If border tax adjustments do not by themselves interfere with efficiency, there is— as far as this goal is concerned—no reason why they should be abolished. If, on the other hand, they operate to reduce potential efficiency, their elimination or modification would be the first step in the right direction. Whereas other inefficiencies may remain, at least this one would be removed. It is, of course, possible that the distortion of efficiency resulting from a certain border tax adjust- ment may happen to offset another distortion, for example, one result- ing from monopoly. In this case, the removal of only one of the two distortions would not be beneficial. However, this is not a valid argument against the elimination of single distortions, for two reasons: (1) such cancellations of several distortions will be a matter of chance, not susceptible to ascertainment,* and (2) the general aim is, as indicated above, to remove the other distortion as well.

The Maximization of Production

The first condition for economic efficiency is that resources in the world be so used that it is impossible to produce more of one commodity without producing less of another. This is, of course, to a large extent a matter of business administration and technology, but production may also be increased by redistributing the employment of factors among different industries.** The second aspect of the problem is of interest in this context.

Two ways are conceivable in which a movement of factors among different industries could increase total production: factor movements within one country, and factor movements from one country to another. The latter will be disregarded for the time being, and international immobility of factors will be assumed. (The special problems arising from international factor movements will be

---

*If the cancellation is intended, e.g., if a particular tax is introduced to counter external diseconomies, the removal of the tax would make no sense. This is a reservation that must be made with respect to all of the following considerations. However, it seems to have only little practical importance in that only few taxes can be so described.

**All firms in one country that produce the same good are here— in their entirety—referred to as an "industry." Maximization of production may also be described as "optimal international division of labor."

considered later in this chapter.) The issue is now, therefore, confined to the following question: How can the movement of a factor from one industry to another within one country increase total world production?

For the reason of brevity, only the factor "labor" is considered in the following examples. However, the conclusions reached are valid for any other productive factor (especially capital) as well. Similarly, only two goods and two countries (A and B) are considered; the results of the analysis are applicable, however, to the realistic case of numerous goods and trading nations.

The effect of a factor movement from one industry to another can only be determined when this movement is isolated and the assumption is made that all other factors remain where they are. This is an extremely simplifying assumption, considering that the demand for factors is a joint demand—joint because different factors interact in producing the final good. Movements of a certain factor will often be accompanied by movements of other factors. However, this assumption makes it possible to measure the effect of factor movements. The conclusions reached in the simple case can be applied as well to the more complex case of various simultaneous factor movements.

Let us assume that in country A six workers leave the car industry and are hired by a piano producer. The effect on piano production will depend upon how much six workers can produce in the piano industry if they are added to the productive factors (capital, labor) already working there.* If output is increased by three pianos, it can be said that the cost of one extra piano in terms of labor is two workers. In economic theory the word "extra" is typically replaced by the word "marginal." Thus, in this case the marginal cost of one piano in terms of labor is two workers.**

The increase in the output of pianos must be accompanied by a decrease in car production. If the marginal cost of a car is assumed to be three workers, the shift of six workers to the piano industry will entail a reduction in output by two cars.

---

*The term "worker" in this and all of the following examples refers to a specific type of worker, i.e., a person with certain skills and experience. The productivity examples must always be seen in relation to a fixed period of time (e.g., one month).

**In this analysis, the term "marginal cost" always refers to a certain factor ("marginal cost in terms of labor"). It does not mean the production cost expressed in dollars but the cost in physical amounts of that factor.

In the situation just described, the ratio in country A between the marginal costs in terms of labor of a piano and of a car is two to three. If we now assume that in country B the marginal cost in terms of labor of one piano is the same as that of one car, the following observation can be made: a shift of six workers from the car industry to the piano industry in A would mean production of two less cars and three more pianos; a shift of labor in B in the opposite direction from the piano industry to the car industry in order to produce two more cars would entail a reduction in the output of pianos by two pianos. Thus, world production of cars would remain unchanged whereas world production of pianos would be increased by one. Obviously, production was not maximized in the situation assumed; it could be increased simply by rearranging the employment of labor between the two industries in both countries.*

Production could not be increased if the ratio between the marginal costs (in terms of labor) of pianos and cars were the same in both countries. For instance, if in A as well as in B the marginal cost of a piano were twice the marginal cost of a car, a shift of labor to the piano industry in A would mean one more piano and two less cars, whereas a shift of labor to the car industry in B would mean two more cars but one less piano.

If these examples—and any others the reader may contrive—are pondered, it becomes obvious that production will only be maximized if the ratio between the marginal costs in terms of labor of producing two goods is the same in all countries.**

What must governments do in order to ensure that production is maximized? Nothing at all. Perfectly competitive factor pricing and free international trade will work together to achieve this result.

Whether workers will shift from one industry to another depends only upon the wage, if free mobility of labor is assumed. In a perfectly competitive market, the wage is not set arbitrarily by the employer but is determined by market forces independent of his will. This can be explained by returning to the example given above. A piano producer hires six additional workers, and as a result three more pianos are

---

*The reason is that in the situation assumed labor in A is relatively more productive in the piano industry and labor in B is relatively more productive in the car industry.

**Except that in this case, labor cannot shift in each country to the industry where it is relatively more productive (compared with the other country), in that the relative productivities are exactly equal.

produced. Each of these six workers will get the same wage. Which wage? Under free competition, the answer is plain. The piano producer will not freely hire six additional men if their aggregate wage exceeds the price of the three pianos they produce.* If, for example, the price of a piano is $1,000, two additional workers are worth $1,000 to the firm. Consequently, the aggregate income of two workers will be $1,000 and the individual wage will be $500.

Now the relationship between marginal costs and commodity prices can be seen. If in country A two additional workers are needed to produce one extra piano and three additional workers are necessary to produce one extra car, the ratio of the marginal costs (in terms of labor) of a piano and a car is two to three. Let us assume that a state of equilibrium exists in A. That means that wages are the same for car workers as for piano workers—otherwise workers would leave their jobs and seek better-paid positions. Therefore, the ratio between the aggregate incomes of the two additional piano workers and the three additional car workers is also two to three. It has been demonstrated in the foregoing paragraph that the aggregate income of the two piano workers is equal to the price of one piano. Similarly, the aggregate income of the three car workers is equal to the price of one car. It follows that the ratio between the price of a piano and that of a car is also two to three. Thus, competitive factor pricing has the consequence that the ratio between the marginal costs (in terms of one factor) is the same as the ratio between the prices of the two goods.

Free trade, i.e., international trade not hampered by tariffs, quotas, and other interferences, means that (if transport costs are neglected) the price of a piano will be uniform in A and B, and the same will be true of the car price. Inasmuch as prices are equal, price ratios are, of course, equal as well. Thus, the fact that in both countries the marginal cost ratio corresponds to the price ratio means that the marginal cost ratio in A and B is the same. It is therefore not possible to increase overall production by shifting factors in different directions in countries A and B. This is the proof that free trade leads to the maximization of production on a global scale. This is one of the specific benefits of free trade. The question whether taxes and border tax adjustments destroy this benefit will be the focus of a later part of this study.

---

*Competition between piano producers will not allow, on the other hand, the price of three pianos to exceed the aggregate wage of six additional workers.

The Optimization of Trade

The second condition for economic efficiency is this: the demands of all consumers must be met in such a way that further international trade could not improve their well-being.*

A consumer will demand and buy an item because he feels it gives him satisfaction or "utility." If he already possesses several units of a good and buys another one, his total utility goes up. The amount of extra utility added by the last unit is commonly referred to as "marginal utility."

The analysis starts from an arbitrary assumption: for the consumers of country A in their entirety, the marginal utility of a piano is three times the marginal utility of a car, whereas for the consumers of B the marginal utility of a piano and that of a car are the same. Total utility in A would increase if A could—by trading with B—give away a car and get a piano in return. Consumers in B would neither lose nor win by that exchange; they attribute the same utility to both goods. Thus, further trade between A and B would increase total welfare. In this case, all of the utility gain would accrue to A. But if it is assumed that for the consumers of B, the marginal utility of a car is twice the marginal utility of a piano (an opposite preference from that existing in A), B would gain as well by the exchange. Other assumptions could be made, but these two examples are sufficient to reveal a fundamental rule: as long as the ratio between the marginal utilities of a piano and a car (or any other two goods) is not the same for consumers in A and in B, total utility can be increased by an exchange of goods between A and B.

If, in contrast, it is assumed that for the consumers of both countries the marginal utility of a piano is twice that of a car, total welfare could not be increased by further trade. If A would receive a piano in exchange for a car, A's gain would exactly be mirrored by B's loss. In this situation, the optimum use of international trade has been made. No further possibility of beneficial trade exists; trade is optimized.

What must a government do in order to ensure the optimization of trade? Nothing at all. The process of rational choice by the consumer and free trade will work together to achieve this result.

The process of rational choice means that a consumer will consider two things when he buys a good: its marginal utility and its

---

*If the condition is fulfilled, international trade will, of course, be used to meet new demand that arises every moment, but it cannot be used to meet the present demand in a better way.

price. In an effort to maximize his well-being, he will arrange his purchases so that every single good is bringing him marginal utility just exactly proportional to its price. If it is now assumed that in country A a situation of equilibrium exists, the fact that the marginal utility of a piano is three times the marginal utility of a car means that the price of a piano must be three times as high as that of a car. (Were it otherwise, consumers would buy more of one good and less of another until equilibrium would be established.) In other words, the ratio of the marginal utilities of a piano and a car is equal to the price ratio.

Inasmuch as free trade makes the price of each good uniform in all countries, price ratios are, of course, equal as well. Thus, the fact that in both countries the marginal utility ratio corresponds to the price ratio means that the marginal utility ratio is the same in A as in B. This is the proof that free trade leads to the optimization of trade, which is its second benefit, the first being the maximization of production. Later discussion will investigate whether taxes and border tax adjustments destroy these benefits.

General Indirect Taxes

At the outset of the analysis, a major dichotomy must be introduced: that between general and selective taxes. General indirect taxes are those that apply to all goods at the same uniform rate. The VAT of the EEC and other countries is the most important example.* Selective indirect taxes, which will be treated later in this chapter, are levied on specific products only.

In the following investigation of the compatibility of a general indirect tax (with and without border adjustments) with economic efficiency, three possible ways to deal with internationally traded goods are considered: the origin principle, the destination principle,

---

*It has been indicated earlier that all VAT countries apply several different rates. For instance, West Germany has a basic rate of 11 percent and a reduced rate of 5.5 percent. The latter, however, applies mainly to agricultural products. Since the EEC abandoned free trade in agricultural goods, this sector poses its own peculiar problems which are not considered here. Other countries apply not only a reduced rate but also an increased rate which usually covers luxuries such as automobiles, television sets, etc. This higher rate may be regarded as a selective tax on luxuries, in addition to the general VAT, and will be considered later.

and combinations of both principles. The origin principle means that internationally traded goods are only liable to indirect tax in the country of origin. All final goods produced in the taxing country, wherever they might be delivered, bear the same tax burden. Under the destination principle, internationally traded goods are liable to indirect tax only in the country of destination. All goods consumed in the taxing country, wherever they might be produced, bear the same tax burden.

In each case it is assumed that only one of the two countries (A) levies a tax whereas in the other country (B) there is no taxation at all of either domestic or internationally traded goods. The results of the analysis can easily be applied to the more complex situation of two taxing countries.

Origin Principle

Price Differences Between A and B. Under the origin principle, a tax is levied on each piano produced in A. No additional tax is due if a piano is exported to B. Competition will not allow piano prices in A and B to differ: someone trying to export a piano to B at a price higher than the domestic price in A would quickly be undersold by a competing exporter. For the same reason, the car price will also be uniform in A and B.*

Maximization of Production. Maximization of production is—in the absence of taxes—achieved by competitive factor pricing and free trade (as shown at the beginning of this chapter). Competitive factor pricing ensures that in every country the ratio between the marginal costs (in terms of a certain factor) of producing two goods is equal to the price ratio of these goods. Free trade equalizes the price ratio everywhere in the world, so that the marginal cost ratios for any two goods are brought in line internationally.

Will the tax impair this beneficial interplay of market forces?

The effect of a general indirect tax on factor pricing can be seen by returning to the previous example. Two extra workers are needed to produce one additional piano, whereas three extra workers are necessary to produce one additional car. The ratio of the marginal costs is two to three. The tax does not cause wages to be different in the two industries (for, if labor is mobile, such differences cannot

---

*The term "price" in this section always means the total price paid by the consumer, i.e., the gross price including tax if any.

persist). Thus, the ratio between the aggregate incomes of two piano workers and three car workers is also two to three. If the piano price is $1,000 and the indirect tax is 10 percent, the piano producer has to pay $100 to the government on each sale and can only pay $900 to the two marginal workers. Thus, the aggregate income of the two piano workers is no longer equal to the piano price but is equal to 90 percent of the piano price.* In the car industry, the effect of the tax is the same: the aggregate income of the three workers is 90 percent of the car price, in that 10 percent is taken away by the government.** Does this change the ratios that are decisive for efficiency? No, in that the ratio between 90 percent of the piano price and 90 percent of the car price is the same as the ratio between the full piano price and the full car price. Consequently, the ratio of the aggregate incomes is still equal to the price ratio (two to three). In other words, the tax does not cause the marginal cost ratio to deviate from the price ratio.

Inasmuch as the price of a piano (or a car) is the same in A as in B, the price ratio continues to be equal in both countries. The tax does not, therefore, impair the maximization of production.

Optimization of Trade. As shown earlier, optimization of trade is, if there are no taxes, achieved by the process of rational choice and by free trade. Rational choice ensures that for every consumer the ratio between the marginal utilities of two goods is equal to their price ratio, whereas free trade means that price ratios are uniform internationally. What will the effect of the tax be on this beneficial interplay of market forces? The tax may cause prices to rise—maybe piano prices more than car prices—but it does not prevent consumers from arranging their purchases in such a way that the marginal utility of each good is proportional to its (gross) price (i.e., price inclusive of the tax). Thus, the marginal utility ratio will continue

---

*This statement is true regardless of the amount by which the tax is shifted forward. In the wake of the first introduction of the tax, the amount of piano production, the piano price, wages, salaries of top management, dividend, and interest paid on capital may all have changed. However, after the adjustment process has ended and equilibrium been re-established, the statement in the text is correct.

**This is true even if the amount of tax shifting in the car industry is quite different from that in the piano industry.

to reflect the price ratio. Inasmuch as the tax does not cause the price ratio in A to differ from that in B, trade continues to be optimized.

Destination Principle

Price Differences Between A and B. Under the destination principle, goods are taxed only in the country where they are consumed. Hence, the price of a piano will be higher in A than in B in that a piano manufactured in A is taxed when it is bought by a consumer in A but not when it is shipped to B. If a 10 percent tax is levied in A, the piano price will be 10 percent higher in A than in B, where we have assumed there are no taxes at all. An exporter who would manage to export pianos from A at the price prevailing there would make a personal profit of 10 percent in that he would either be exempted from paying the tax or get the tax refunded. Therefore, competition among exporters will force the export price down until it reaches a level exactly 10 percent below A's price.* Similarly, competition will establish a 10 percent price difference if pianos are imported into A from B. On the basis of the same considerations, A's car price will exceed B's car price by 10 percent.

Maximization of Production. The effect of the tax on factor pricing is this: if the piano price in A is $1,000, the piano producer in A will pay $100 on each domestic sale to the government and $900 will accrue to the productive factors. For each piano exported to B, the producer gets $900; this is the piano price prevailing in B. No tax is due on exports, and thus each piano means $900 for the factors of production (i.e., 90 percent of the piano price in A), regardless of whether it is exported or not. The same is true in the case of cars, so that in A the ratio of the aggregate incomes of two piano workers and three car workers is again equal to the price ratio.

The price ratio in A does not differ from that in B; both the car price and the piano price in B are exactly 90 percent of the respective prices in A. It follows that production is maximized.

---

*This has nothing to do with the question of whether the tax in A has after its introduction been shifted forward or not. Even if it had been shifted only partially into final prices, exporters would be able (and would, therefore, by competition be forced) to sell at prices 10 percent below domestic prices.

Optimization of Trade. The tax in A does not prevent consumers
from arranging their purchases in such a way that the ratio of
marginal utilities equals the price ratio. Inasmuch as the price
ratio in B is the same as in A, trade is optimized.

Taxation of Intermediate Goods

Uniformity of the Tax Rate on Final Goods. It has been assumed in
the preceding discussions that under a 10 percent general indirect
tax, 10 percent of the final price of any good will accrue to the
government and 90 percent will be paid to the factors of production.
On reflection, the validity of this assumption turns out to depend upon
the taxation of intermediate goods (inputs). If, for example, there is
a general indirect tax of 2 percent on all purchased goods, intermediate
and final, the car producer not only pays 2 percent of the final car
price to the state but he also uses a part of the final price to purchase
inputs, and on each of these purchases again 2 percent is paid to the
state. The portion of the final price that in effect ends up in the state's
treasury may be about 10 percent.* But because it depends on the
amount of intermediate purchases, it may well be 8 percent in the car
industry and 12 percent in the piano industry. In this case, the ratios
that are decisive for the maximization of production would no longer
correspond. Similarly, trade would not be optimized if, in the case
of the destination principle, the percentage of tax saving would not be
exactly the same on each exported good.** Therefore, the statement

---

*This means that about 90 percent of the price paid by the
consumer for a car accrues to the factors that have produced that
car. In the example given above—three workers are needed to produce
one marginal car—the purchase of inputs by the car producer has
for the sake of simplicity not been mentioned. The example is valid
if the production of inputs is not regarded as a separate industry but
as a part of the manufacturing process of the final good. For instance,
the coal industry must be thought to be divided into many tiny segments,
each being a part of the industry that uses coal in its production
process.

**The definition of "industry" given in the preceding footnote
shows that implementation of the pure destination principle means
exemption of exports from all taxes. No input used in the manufacturing process, not even fuel and similar auxiliary materials, may
be taxed, so that the entire final price accrues to the productive
factors. A less comprehensive tax exemption means that a mixture
of the destination and origin principles will be implemented.

that a general indirect tax does not interfere with efficiency is only true if intermediate goods are not taxed at all or if they are taxed in such a way that the percentage of the final price taken away by the government from the productive factors is the same in all industries. The most important types of general indirect taxes, the VAT and the retail sales tax, fulfill this condition.

Importation of Intermediate Goods. How should country A tax imported intermediate goods used by its car industry (e.g., imported steel)? The considerations in the preceding section provide the answer. It may be assumed that in A each purchase of a good (intermediate as well as final) is taxed in a way that the total tax burden on the final product is 10 percent (this is a proper description of a VAT). If the purchase of an imported intermediate good remains untaxed, it seems that the total tax will amount to a smaller percentage of the final price and that consequently the "wedge" the tax drives between the final price and the aggregate income of the marginal workers will be smaller than 10 percent. However, this is only true if the exported good that in fact paid for the imported steel was not taxed. For the purpose of ascertaining the marginal cost of car production in A, the car industry must be imagined to include that portion of A's export industry which is necessary to pay for the steel imports.* This means that if a tax is put on the exports exchanged for foreign steel, this tax is in effect paid by the car producer. Therefore, country A may either tax imported intermediate goods or tax all exports; in both cases production will be maximized. It follows that under the origin principle (i.e., taxation of exports) there should be no tax on imported inputs, whereas under the destination principle (i.e., no taxation of exports) imported inputs should be taxed in exactly the same way as domestic inputs.

Exportation of Intermediate Goods. Maximization of production should be achieved for all goods produced in a country that are either consumed there or exported. Therefore, the condition of maximized production should be applied to exported intermediate goods as well as to finished products. It follows from the analysis in the preceding discussions that under the origin principle exported inputs should be taxed at the same rate as exported finished goods, whereas under the destination principle, no exports—whether intermediate or final products—should be taxed.

Combinations of the Destination
and Origin Principles

Different Principles for Exports and Imports. If imports are subject

---

*This is a further extension of the term "industry."

to the destination principle and exports subject to the origin principle, the effect is that both exports and imports are taxed. If country A exports pianos and imports cars, the piano price will be uniform whereas the car price will be higher in A than in B. This means that neither maximization of production nor optimization of trade is achieved.

Different Principles for Different Goods. If country A, which generally adheres to the origin principle, introduces the destination principle for cars only, the effect is the same as in the preceding case.

Different Principles for Trade with Different Countries. If country A adopts the destination principle for its trade with country B but the origin principle vis-à-vis country C, the latter will try to import A's goods through B, thus avoiding A's tax. If this evasion is made impossible by rules of origin, economic efficiency will be reduced, as can be seen by an adaptation of the example given in the previous case to a three-country situation. The same is true if the border adjustment rate of A is different vis-à-vis different countries. Therefore, an objection must be raised to the proposal made by an official of the International Fiscal Association that countries complaining about the present border tax adjustments should seek to conclude bilateral treaties with their trading partners incorporating border tax rules, instead of waiting endlessly for a multinational consensus.[3] Such bilateral treaties could, if they did not provide for most-favored-nation treatment, create new economic inefficiencies. A multilateral approach, using the GATT channels, is preferable.

Partial Implementation of Either Principle for All Trade. If country A levies a 10 percent VAT and applies border tax adjustments (import taxes and export rebates) of 5 percent, it subjects international trade to a mixture of destination principle (which would mean 10 percent border adjustments) and origin principle (which would mean zero border adjustments). The analysis used earlier can be used to determine the compatibility of such a system with economic efficiency. Again, prices in A will exceed prices in B by the same percentage in the case of each commodity (here 5 percent). Trade will thus be optimized. Further, the net price received by producers in A from their domestic sales and their exports will again be the same; it will be equal to A's price minus the tax, which is the same as B's price minus the difference between the tax and the tax rebate. Therefore, production will be maximized.

Result

A general indirect tax does not interfere with economic efficiency, whether it is applied on an origin basis or on a destination basis.[4]

Even a mixture of the two systems is admissible, provided that export rebates and import taxes are at the same rate for all goods. It would be incorrect, therefore, to think that border tax adjustments that reflect the actual amount of tax shifting would be preferable with respect to economic efficiency. On the contrary, such adjustments would have to distinguish between different goods, in that the amount of shifting varies from industry to industry. The discussion above of "Different Principles for Different Goods" demonstrated that this would reduce efficiency.

Selective Indirect Taxes

Selective indirect taxes are those which do not apply to all or almost all goods but only to selected products. Whereas the importance of general indirect taxes is obvious in that the VAT qualifies as such a tax, the significance of selective indirect taxes requires closer investigation.

It is natural to think first of the traditional excises, especially on petroleum products, alcohol, and tobacco, which provide a considerable part of the total tax revenue in all EEC countries.[5] However, it must be realized that these excises usually have quite peculiar properties: they are levied at an extremely high rate, they involve goods for which the demand is rather inelastic,* and in many cases they show great resemblance to a tariff in that they are applied to goods manufactured from raw material which is almost exclusively imported by the taxing country.** In considering traditional excises, therefore, the conclusions drawn from the following analysis must be qualified by special considerations taking account of these peculiarities (see "Preliminary Conclusions" in this chapter; also see Chapter 5).

Another significant group of selective indirect taxes, usually overlooked in this context, can be seen in the increased rates that most countries with a general indirect tax apply to certain products.

---

*Tea and coffee are other examples, in addition to the three main excises mentioned above.

**For instance, in the two EEC countries with the highest excises, Italy and West Germany, 70 to 80 percent of the excise tax revenue is derived from taxation of goods made of tobacco and petroleum, materials not produced to a significant extent in these countries. A similar effect could be achieved by tariffs on these imported materials.

It has already been pointed out that such an increased tax rate amounts
to the imposition of a special tax in addition to the general tax. As a
rule, luxury items are subject to the increased rate, and these goods
are commonly important objects of mutual international trade, especiall
between the industrial countries. The French VAT may serve as an
example. Whereas the normal rate for all goods is 23 percent,* a
special rate of 33 1/3 percent applies to new automobiles, cameras,
films, radio and television sets, tape recorders, furs, and a few other
items.[6] Most VAT countries have similar increased rates.

A third group of selective indirect taxes, much more closely
related to the second group than to the traditional excises, is provided
by countries that do not have a general indirect tax but levy taxes on
specific goods other than the traditional excise commodities. Japan
is the prime example among the industrialized countries. It applies
a tax to about two thirds of all products, with rates ranging from 5
percent to 40 percent. The highest rates are for goods similar to
those covered by the increased rates in the VAT countries (e.g.,
automobiles). The British purchase tax and some of the U.S. federal
excises (again, automobiles provide the most significant example)
also belong to this group of selective indirect taxes.

Origin Principle

If country A puts a tax on cars but not on pianos (because it
wants to fight pollution but to foster the arts), the origin principle
ensures that the car price in A (just as the piano price) does not differ
from that in B, in that cars can still be freely imported from B.
Therefore, trade continues to be optimized. The tax in A drives a
"wedge" between the price and the aggregate income of the marginal
workers in the car industry but not in the piano industry, so that in
A the price ratio no longer mirrors the marginal cost ratio. The
price ratio in B, where no tax is levied, is of course equal to the
marginal cost ratio there, so that the ratios of the marginal costs of
producing a piano and a car differ in the two countries. Consequently,
production is not maximized.

Destination Principle

A tax levied in A on cars but not on pianos means now that
the price of a car is higher in A than in B while the piano price

---

*Two different reduced rates of 7.5 percent and 17.6 percent
are applied mainly to food products. It has already been pointed out
that reduced rates of this kind can be disregarded for the purpose
of this book.

continues to be uniform. Trade is no longer optimized. The car price in A exceeds the aggregate income of the marginal car workers by the tax rate. Similarly, the car price in A exceeds the car price in B by the tax rate. Therefore, the aggregate income of the marginal car workers in A is equal to the car price in B. Inasmuch as there is no tax on pianos, the ratio between the aggregate incomes of the marginal workers in the car and piano industries in A (which is equal to the marginal cost ratio in A) mirrors the price ratio in B (which is equal to the marginal cost ratio in B). As a consequence, production is maximized.

Result

Under the origin principle, trade is optimized but production is not maximized. Under the destination principle, the reverse is true. The two efficiency conditions are opposed to each other. A solution to this conflict will be elaborated below and in Chapter 5.

General Direct Taxes

The question whether border tax adjustments for direct taxes would enhance economic efficiency is of particular importance in that such adjustments are presently not made but are frequently demanded. Only income taxes are considered, as the prime example of direct taxation. The term "general" income tax refers to a tax that applies to the income of a certain factor regardless of the industry in which it works. It need not be general in other respects: it may apply different rates to the incomes earned by different factors, and it may be a progressive income tax, i.e., the rate may increase with the income earned by the factor. Under such a general income tax, a particular factor will not be encouraged for income tax reasons to move to another industry. A "selective" income tax, on the other hand, is one that discriminates against the use of a factor in a particular industry. The factor's income is taxed at a different rate in different industries, e.g., income from capital is taxed at a lower rate if this capital is invested in the shipbuilding industry. This section deals with general income taxes, the next with selective income taxes. The focus is on the income tax as it is presently applied, that is, without border adjustments.

Maximization of Production

If income is taxed, equilibrium will be established only if the net income of a certain factor is the same in all industries. Therefore, the ratio of the marginal costs in terms of labor for two goods equals the ratio of the aggregate net incomes of the marginal workers. If an income tax of 10 percent is levied, the aggregate net income of the two workers needed to produce one extra piano is 90 percent of the piano price. Even under a progressive income tax, the rate applied to the income of the same workers in the car industry is also 10 percent; the underlying assumption is that the specific workers who are considered earn the same net income in all industries. Therefore, the ratio between the aggregate net incomes of the marginal workers in the two industries is equal to the price ratio, and production is maximized.

Optimization of Trade

A general income tax imposed in country A does nothing to cause the price of a particular product to differ in A and B. It does nothing, therefore, to disturb the optimization of trade. This statement is independent of what one assumes about the shifting of the tax. Prices in A might increase as a result of the tax, and they might increase to a different extent for different goods, but the competitive forces will not tolerate a price difference between A and B, and adjustment will take place until prices are uniform again.

Result

A general income tax does not interfere with maximum efficiency of the world economy. If the income tax were rebated on exports, the result would probably be different price ratios in A and B.* This would interfere with the optimization of trade, and nothing would thereby be gained for economic efficiency—the result would be the contrary. Therefore, a general income tax produces no argument in favor of imposing border tax adjustments.

Selective Direct Taxes

If country A decides to tax the incomes of workers in the car industry but not in the piano industry (in order, for example, to make a dying piano industry more attractive for productive factors), prices

---

*The reason is that the rate of rebate would differ from product to product, in that the ratio between income tax and sales revenue differs from export industry to export industry.

for both goods will nevertheless be uniform in both countries (i.e., trade is optimized). The tax drives a "wedge" between the price and the aggregate net income of the marginal workers in the car industry but not in the piano industry, so that maximization of production is not achieved.

Production can be maximized by means of border tax adjustments. What is necessary is to bring the ratio of the marginal costs in country A in line with B's price ratio. If the income tax in A favors a selected industry by applying a lower rate, this effect can be achieved by taxing the exports of the favored industry and subsidizing imports of the same product. However, the price to be paid would be interference with the optimization of trade. The following discussion, and that in Chapter 5, will investigate which of the two conflicting results— maximization of production or optimization of trade—is preferable.

TAX CHANGES AND THE BALANCE OF PAYMENTS

The Policy Goal: Independence of the Balance of Payments from Domestic Tax Changes

Whereas the first broad policy goal considered here—that taxes should not interfere with the conditions for maximum efficiency of the world economy—requires little justification, the second goal—that the balance of payments should not be influenced by domestic tax changes—is not universally accepted.

Question No. 1

Why, it has been asked, should the effect of taxes, of all things, be neutralized when every other aspect of national economic policy as well as numerous additional domestic developments and circumstances influence the balance of payments to a large extent?[7] To answer this question the following observation should be made: If the ratio between a country's exports and its imports becomes smaller and this results in a permanent deficit in the balance of payments, only certain kinds of measures are available to the country threatened by the possible adverse effects such a deficit may have on its domestic economy:*

---

*The following considerations and conclusions apply, mutatis mutandis, also to the case of a surplus in the balance of payments, but with the qualification that a deficit is more dangerous for a country than a surplus.

1. Countermeasures of domestic economic policy. This may be a thorny or even unacceptable means of adjustment in that the goals of foreign and domestic economic policy may be conflicting.

2. Interference with free trade, by raising tariffs, imposing quotas, restricting foreign travel, subsidizing exports, etc. Even disregarding the well-known adverse effect on economic efficiency, action of this kind, if it affects trade in goods and services, is generally ruled out by international law except for emergency measures, the very nature of which is their temporariness (see GATT Article XIX— "Emergency Action").

3. Devaluation of the country's currency. This possibility could sometimes provide a simple answer to balance of payments difficulties.* But for a variety of reasons,** most countries are so reluctant to effect a parity change that they would rather resort to all kinds of alternative measures in order to avoid it, even if these measures lead to economic inefficiency and violation of international law.

4. Imposition of duties on imports and simultaneous subsidization of exports at the same rate. Although such a system seems to lend itself to undesirable exploitation (differentiation between various goods or countries, unlimited increase of the rate over the years) and is, therefore, generally ruled out by international law,[8] there is one way to confine its development without arbitrariness: it can be merged inseparably with national indirect taxes. Such mergers of border adjustments and domestic taxes have been approved, after long historical development, by international law.

Whereas the first three measures may be used to neutralize influences of all kinds on the balance of payments, the international trading community has not yet sanctioned introduction of levy/subsidy schemes unconnected with internal indirect taxes. There appears to be no rational way to link such a system to any phenomenon of the national

----

*The effect of a devaluation on the balance of payments, especially on the trade balance, depends largely upon the domestic economic situation in the devaluing country.

**Ranging from genuine concern about the effects on the domestic economy to national pride, position as a world banker, domestic pressure groups worrying about their foreign investment or foreign debt, or special considerations like the EEC farm policy which is seriously disrupted by a member country's parity change.

economy other than a tax.* The proposal to go one step further and allow schemes of this kind to be implemented whenever the balance of payments demands it, without regard to certain domestic factors, has been made with increasing frequency in recent years[9] but has proved to be too radical a departure from traditional lines for the wary international organization that establishes the rules for parity changes—the International Monetary Fund (IMF).

The answer to the introductory question is, therefore, as simple as it is disappointing to someone who would rather disregard the clumsy instruments of international economic policy that are available to today's politicians and establish a utopian order: Any circumstance that entails a serious disequilibrium in the balance of payments may require corrective action. However, international consensus restricts the range of sanctioned countervailing measures, and a permanent levy/subsidy scheme is, wisely or not, allowed only in connection with indirect taxes. The fact that a system of this kind is not allowed to counterweigh effects other than those of taxes furnishes no reason to denounce the scheme for taxes as well and take recourse to the first three measures. The choice is not between allowing no countervailing measures for any influences on the balance of payments and approving a levy/subsidy system for taxes only—as the introductory question misleadingly implies. Rather, the choice is between allowing general adjustments (especially parity changes) for all influences whatsoever and permitting in addition a special adjustment, made to measure, for tax influences. Faced with this latter choice, there is no reason to vote for the first alternative.

The question whether a levy/subsidy system should be sanctioned in order to provide an adjustment for all possible circumstances influencing the balance of payments is not a subject of this book. The following discussions only investigate whether a system of this kind is a useful instrument in dealing with balance of payments problems entailed by domestic tax changes, whether it should be applied to indirect taxes only or to direct taxes as well, and how exactly it should be administered. The touchstone used in this investigation will be the independence of a country's trade balance of all changes in its tax system. This provokes yet another question.

---

*A levy/subsidy system could, of course, be linked to the country's balance of payments situation, just as today parity changes are linked to it (under the International Monetary Fund Agreement, exchange rate alterations are only permitted in certain kinds of disequilibrium). But this would mean that the levy/subsidy rates were not limited and could increase tremendously over the decades. This would be undesirable (see "Indirect Taxation and International Factor Movements," in this chapter).

Question No. 2

Why should the balance of payments be prevented from moving, as the result of a domestic tax increase or decrease, from its previous surplus or deficit, as it may be, into equilibrium? The answer is again as simple as it is disappointing to someone seeking an ideal solution: consideration of a general levy/subsidy system is omitted in this book, and so is an investigation of the question whether such a system should perhaps be introduced in the guise of flexible border tax adjustments. If, e.g., actual application of border adjustments equalizing the deficit-producing effect of a tax change were tied to the taxing country's balance of payments situation, the result would be the following:[10] Country A, already in deficit, would apply the adjustments; country B, presently in surplus, would not. If B would later move into a deficit, it would make up for its previous omission of border adjustments. A rule prohibiting such a belated application of the adjustments would not be acceptable to B, considering that A was allowed to equalize for its domestic tax burden when it faced a deficit, and that B, had it not omitted the adjustments in the first place, would not have run into a deficit. Similarly, if A would enjoy a surplus at a later time, it would have to abandon the border adjustments it had adopted earlier. Again, another rule would not be acceptable to B in that it did in the first place what A is supposed to do now: remove the surplus by accepting (instantly or belatedly) the deficit-producing effect of the tax change. Such a system of retarding the effects of domestic tax changes until they are appropriate or re-establishing them in order to achieve a balance of payments equilibrium is, of course, nothing other than a disguised general levy/subsidy scheme. The circumstances equalized in their impact on the balance of payments are not taxes but all the other factors that influence this balance.

Apart from the argument that the label "tax adjustment" would be entirely inappropriate for such a system, another objection to it must be raised (if it is limited to indirect taxes, as the present border tax adjustments are): countries with high indirect taxes are given a full scope adjustment mechanism, whereas other countries can use only a small margin of perhaps a few percentage points, which may not be sufficient to correct a disequilibrium.

The following investigation will, therefore, be narrow in a way that is similar to the limitation of the foregoing considerations (compatibility of border tax adjustments with economic efficiency). The effects of taxes are isolated, and only a solution to the problems posed by taxes themselves is attempted. In the foregoing section, economic inefficiencies resulting from other causes were neglected in that their removal is a different, independent task. In the following

reasoning, effects of circumstances other than taxes on the balance
of payments will be disregarded. Equalization of such effects is
another important task for the policy-maker. To make the balance
of payments independent from domestic taxation is a first significant
step. It cannot be said that future tax changes without border tax
adjustments would, more often than not, move the balance of payments
toward equilibrium.* This would be entirely a matter of chance, and
an occasional good effect achieved by the blind forces of coincidence
is no valid reason for favoring a system in which mere chance would
bring some good and many bad results over a system in which domestic
tax increases or decreases would leave the balance of international
payments entirely unchanged.

If complete exchange rate flexibility were achieved in the future,
a special system for tax changes would perhaps become unnecessary.
The general arrangement would then absorb the special one, and this
discussion of the balance of payments would (in contrast to the foregoing and the following sections) become partly obsolete. However,
it is unlikely that freely floating exchange rates will be agreed upon
in the near and even in the more distant future. Rather, a compromise
between exchange rate stability and flexibility will be sought.** The
remaining stability, whatever its extent may be, will still make it
desirable for countries to possess a special system preventing any

---

*It is, of course, tempting to base one's conclusions on the
present situation which in fact suggests that European countries, by
raising their indirect taxes even further, would reduce their balance
of payments surplus vis-à-vis the United States, if no border adjustments were employed. However, surpluses and deficits are subject
to change over the decades, whereas international rules of this kind
tend to have a long life—simply because international consensus is
not easily reached. The adoption of the GATT rules on border adjustments in 1947 should be a forbidding example. The United States
enjoyed a big surplus in the payments balance at that time, and the
GATT rules were thought to help the European countries overcome
the dollar shortage. This shows how dangerous it is to consider only
a specific situation while pondering adoption of a rule rather than
working out an arrangement that yields satisfactory results in all
possible situations.

**Some measure of flexibility is provided even today in that
currencies are allowed to deviate from the parity by up to 2.25 percent
to either side (the margin was widened from 1 percent to 2.25 percent
in 1971).

influences of tax changes on the balance of payments. Consideration of such a system is, therefore, still a worthwhile task.

Four kinds of domestic tax changes will be considered separately: increase of an indirect tax, increase of a direct tax, substitution of an indirect for a direct tax, and tax decreases. In each case, the question will be the following: How should internationally traded goods be taxed in order to keep the balance of payments undisrupted by the domestic change?

Increase of a General Indirect Tax[11]

Origin Principle

If wages are not flexible, prices will rise as the supply curve shifts upward. This means that exports will decline and foreign products will gain attractiveness over high-priced domestic goods. If the government spends all of the new tax revenue, aggregate demand will increase and the deficit-producing effect on the trade balance caused by the price rise will be aggravated. If private and public spending propensities are the same, the price rise is the only primary cause leading to a deficit. Two other developments can be observed:

1. The rise in prices increases the transaction demand for money, and, assuming a fixed money supply, the interest rate goes up.* The resulting decline in investment expenditures reduces income and consumption via the familiar multiplier process. A decrease in imports is the consequence.

2. The balance of payments deficit and the income reduction may tend to retard the rate of wage increases in comparison with other countries, so that the exports will gradually rise again. This point (the only one directly related to the problem of "tax shifting") is hotly disputed. The opinion that wages will decelerate is, for example, maintained by Robert E. Baldwin (with a hint at the Phillips curve),[12] it is doubted by Musgrave,[13] and the reverse—a tendency for wages to increase even more—is assumed by Walter Salant.[14]

Whatever one assumes about these two points, the primary, deficit-producing effect of the price rise is likely to prevail.

---

*The interest rate is, of course, greatly manipulated by government action. But the analysis tries to isolate the effects of the tax change itself, because the objective is to neutralize these effects on the balance of payments, rather than the effects of any simultaneous government action.

Destination Principle

The price rise is limited to domestically consumed goods, so that no immediate, heavy impact on the trade balance comparable to that observed under the origin principle results. Among the more subtle effects of the tax rise, those tending to create a surplus and those leading to a deficit must, again, be distinguished:

1. The rise in prices tends to increase the interest rate, thereby cutting investment and reducing real income. Imports decrease consequently. The decline in domestic output will, when upward-sloping supply curves are assumed, reduce costs and, therefore, export prices. All this would move the balance of payments into surplus, if there were no countervailing forces.

2. If the government chooses to spend all of the new tax revenue—and it is not unlikely that it will—total demand increases, which leads to still higher prices, more imports, and higher production costs. The effect will be to move the balance of payments toward a deficit.

3. The long-term effect of the domestic price rise on wages is not clearly determinable; deficit and surplus tendencies are intertwined.

The aggregate effect on the balance of payments will vary according to the present monetary and fiscal policy prevailing in the taxing country. Neither a big deficit nor a big surplus seems to be likely, however, compared with the magnitude of the probable effect of the origin principle.[15] Therefore, the destination principle is preferable to the origin principle.

Increase of a Direct Tax

In this context, attention can be confined to the corporate profit tax. Although personal income taxes are generally more important in terms of revenue yield, border adjustments for them have never seriously been demanded because little or no forward shifting seems to be likely. Whether an increase in the corporate profit tax raises prices is a much debated issue. If there is such a price effect, a levy/subsidy system would have to be introduced in the case of a tax increase in order to neutralize the resulting impact on the trade balance.

The main proponent of the view that the corporate income tax is substantially or even entirely shifted forward into prices is Harvard economist Richard A. Musgrave.[16] Extensive studies led him to this belief after he had earlier held the opinion that, according to theoretical reasoning as well as empirical observation, about one third of the tax must be considered as being shifted into prices.[17]

Recent empirical studies do not support the thesis of 100 percent shifting but, on the contrary, conclude that the traditional view of almost no shifting is correct.18 The issue must be regarded as unsettled, a fact that dampens enthusiasm for border adjustments that adjust for price effects of corporate income taxes.

The question is, of course, whether the whole problem is a very important one. In the industrial countries, permanent increases in corporate profit taxes are already less frequent and smaller than increases in indirect taxes. The reasons for this phenomenon have been indicated in Chapter 1. Future tax increases will probably more and more focus on the field of indirect taxation. Direct taxation as a percentage of GNP is at present rather similar in the developed countries, and this is not very likely to change, for reasons also already indicated. This suggests that the need to neutralize the impact of direct taxes on the trade balance is considerably smaller than in the case of indirect taxation. Given the total obscurity of the price effect of these taxes, it seems preferable to include them in the large group of circumstances in respect to which only general adjustments for international trade are made, such as the presently available measures or any future means of exchange rate flexibility.

Tax Decreases

In spite of what is called the "law of ever-increasing government activity," tax decreases do sometimes occur. In the case of direct taxes, a corresponding lowering of prices has not been observed.19 A decrease in indirect taxes which are separately shown on invoices (this is the mechanism of the VAT) is more likely to be reflected in lower gross prices, in that net prices which are known to the purchaser will rather tend to remain unchanged. The soundness of the result that the destination principle should be adopted for changes in indirect taxes but no border adjustments should be made for direct taxes (suggested in preceding discussions) is confirmed by this observation.

Substitution of an Indirect
Tax for a Direct Tax

This is a special case of introducing or increasing an indirect tax. Inasmuch as it occurred several times in the past (e.g., the 1969 tax reform in Norway) and is contemplated in some countries for the future (United States, West Germany), the result achieved in the above section "Increase of General Indirect Tax" must be judged in this context. The result was that an increase in indirect taxation should be accompanied by adjustments implementing the destination principle rather than the origin principle.

The uncertainty about the shifting of profit taxes is mirrored, of course, in an uncertainty about the price effects of a change of this kind. It is obvious that the analysis would be the same as that in "Destination Principle," supra, if the direct tax were not reflected in prices at all. But what should be concluded if full shifting of the direct tax is assumed?

As already indicated, such shifting can only be assumed for a corporate profit tax, and therefore only a changeover from this tax to an indirect tax gives rise to special problems. Whether a general price rise results from such a changeover, and to what extent, depends upon the price effect of the profit tax reduction, which, as already shown, is likely to be small. It can hardly be assumed that the change-over leaves prices unchanged; in a time of continuous upward pressure on prices, business will take the opportunity and avail itself of the excuse of "new taxes" for substantial price rises. This has occurred in the case of European countries which substituted a VAT for cumulative turnover taxes[20] or direct taxes. In any event, inasmuch as un-incorporated business contributes heavily to the value of consumer goods, prices will rise for this reason. The secondary effect, a wage increase, is likely to follow in the wake of a rise in the consumer price index, setting into motion the wage-price spiral.

For these reasons, adoption of the origin principle for the new indirect tax would very likely affect the trade balance in the direction of a deficit. The destination principle would mitigate that effect. If a surplus should result from the latter principle, it will tend to disappear in the long run: imports are taxed under the destination principle, and their prices go up relative to domestic prices as far as the latter are not increased by the amount of the indirect tax. This entails a further increase in the consumer price index, with its possible wage effects. Apart from that, the shift of domestic demand away from imports will raise domestic output and increase real income, effects which put a deficit pressure on the balance of payments.

INDIRECT TAXATION AND INTERNATIONAL FACTOR MOVEMENTS

Definition of the Issue

International Mobility of Factors of Production

At the beginning of this chapter, in the consideration of the impact of taxes on economic efficiency, the factors of production were assumed to be unable to move from one country to another. International immobility of factors is, however, not verified by empirical observation; the facts indicate the contrary. The flow of private capital from the United States to foreign countries, for example, is a major reason why the American trade surplus is canceled out in the overall balance of payments. On the other hand, it would certainly be grossly incorrect to assume perfect factor mobility internationally. The question arises, therefore, to what extent factor movements from one country to another should be taken into account in a study of border tax adjustments.

A basic distinction must be drawn between common markets on the one hand and countries not united by such economic integration on the other. In a common market, not only high mobility of capital but also considerable mobility of labor between the member states can develop, depending upon many circumstances and especially the degree of actual integration. One example is provided by the common labor market of the Scandinavian countries—Denmark, Finland, Norway, and Sweden—which has existed since 1953. Considerable migration of workers from Finland to Sweden has been reported. Another, more recent example is the European Economic Community. The continuing drive toward intensified integration in the EEC is likely to foster migration of workers and increase capital mobility. For countries lacking this kind of cooperation, however, only the factor capital can be assumed to possess mobility of a significant degree. International movements of labor are rarely observed to an extent that would merit consideration in the context of taxation. Nevertheless, such movements do occur in special situations—e.g., between Canada and the United States, from Yugoslavia and Spain to West Germany, from many southern European countries to Switzerland. The following investigation, although explicitly excluding the special problems of common markets, will, therefore, address itself not only to capital but also to labor movements. The relatively minor significance of the latter must be kept in mind in order to put the problems in perspective.

Direct Taxes, Indirect Taxes, and International Factor Movements: The Two Fields of International Tax Law

Direct Taxes. The impact of direct taxes on international factor movements is a subject that has been prominent among economists and especially among lawyers for a long time. Double taxation and tax evasion are catchwords for the problems that troubled many countries almost from the very introduction of the income tax as a major revenue source. Factor movements induced by income tax differentials are one facet of this many-sided area. As early as 1920, the League of Nations began to study possibilities for international cooperation in the field of income taxes. A surge of bilateral treaties for the avoidance of double taxation and the prevention of fiscal evasion resulted. A wealth of legal studies exists in this area, which is often referred to as "International Tax Law."21

Thus far the analysis in this chapter has led to the conclusion that no border tax adjustments should be introduced for general direct taxes and that no consideration of the impact of such adjustments on factor movements is necessary. What remains is the question whether direct taxes, as they are presently administered (that is, without border adjustments), create inefficiencies with regard to international flows of capital and labor—a question that is not a subject of this book, in that inefficiencies of this kind cannot be redressed by a special tax treatment of internationally traded goods but only (if at all) by a certain taxation of incomes that are related in some way to factors or persons which move from one country to another.

Indirect Taxes. International aspects of indirect taxation have been unduly overshadowed by the prominence of income tax laws and conventions. Treatises on international tax law usually do not even touch the subject of indirect taxes. However, with the universal advance of this kind of taxation (see Chapter 1) the importance of the problems it poses internationally is bound to increase, and future treatises of the kind just mentioned will either have to change their title or include this new field of international tax law.

Despite apparent analogy, the questions arising in the two fields differ to a great extent. One of the common issues is the consideration of international factor movements that might be the consequence of certain features of the domestic tax law.22

Different Causes of Factor Movements Distinguished

In the following analysis it will be assumed that, before the introduction of the general indirect tax,* the international distribution of factors is optimal (not in the sense of utopian economic efficiency,

---

*Only general indirect taxes are considered in this analysis. A selective indirect tax may induce factor movements, but the domestic economy will usually be large enough to absorb or provide these factors, and the impact on the international factor distribution can be assumed to be so minor that it does not warrant consideration.

but in the sense of maximum efficiency attainable given the actual
degree of international mobility of factors).23 This assumption is
necessary in order to isolate the detrimental effects of the tax, if
there are any. A flow of factors caused by the tax will change this
optimal distribution, if there are no offsetting circumstances.

The introduction of an indirect tax can produce international
factor movements simply because of the reduction in real income it
entails. (Domestic prices rise, but money incomes remain unchanged.)
Further movements can result from a change in the balance of payments which may follow in the wake of the new domestic tax. Additional
factor flows can be caused by the destination principle, in that the
import levies and tax rebates result in a general price difference for
all products (investment as well as consumption goods) between the
taxing country and the rest of the world.

The following considerations will focus on a general indirect
tax which implements the destination principle, inasmuch as the
analysis of this chapter thus far has shown this to be preferable to
the origin principle for general indirect taxes. It is therefore the
third possibility (factor movements caused by the levy/subsidy system
of the destination principle) that is of special interest here. The
second possibility can be largely ignored in this context in that balance
of payment changes under the destination principle are only minor
and their direction is not predictable. The first possibility—factor
movements caused by the negative income effect of a tax—neither
results from nor can it be removed merely by a special tax treatment of internationally traded goods. Its consideration is, therefore,
outside the scope of this study. Factor flows of this kind are here
regarded as an inevitable price to be paid for national taxation.

Investigation Confined to the Destination Principle

The second of the three possibilities is significant in the case
of the origin principle, in that a considerable deficit in the balance
of payments must be expected to result from a domestic tax increase.
Such a deficit will, in the long run, give rise to international factor
flows.24 However, the following analysis will be confined to the
destination principle, because the question to be asked here is not
which one is preferable, the origin or the destination principle. Both
of these principles give rise to some international factor flows, for
different reasons. It is impossible to compare the magnitude of the
resulting welfare changes. Thus, it is impossible to decide which of
the two principles is preferable in this respect, and the previous
result (superiority of the destination principle) remains unchallenged.
The question which is asked here is, therefore, the following: Of
what kind are the welfare costs of the destination principle with respect

to international factor flows? The answer to this question must be
known at least approximately if an overall evaluation of the destination
principle is attempted.

International Factor Movements Caused
by the Levy/Subsidy System of the Destination
Principle

The Model

In order to isolate the effects of the levy subsidy system (which
is necessary to implement the destination principle) from the other
effects of taxes, the following assumption is made: The real income
of labor is the same in A as in B. The interest rate on capital is
also the same in the two countries. Initially, no country applies
border tax adjustments, and, therefore, under idealized conditions
of free trade without transport costs, the price level is the same as
well. Under these circumstances, no inducement for factor movements
exists.

If A subjects its international trade to border tax adjustments
of 15 percent (a realistic figure today), the price level in A will be
higher than that in B by the same percentage. The identity of real
labor income and of the rate of capital interest in A and B is, however,
still assumed. Will factors tend to move internationally in this
situation?

Capital Flows

No inducement exists for capital flows from B to A; the interest
rate is the same. If capital moves from A to B, however, an advantage
seems to result: inasmuch as the price level in B is lower by 15
percent, the capital owner in A is able to buy investment goods in B
at a considerably lower price than he would have to pay in A. It is
less expensive for him, therefore, to build an equivalent factory in
B than in A. However, the apparent advantage is nullified when the
income from the factory is transferred to A or the factory is finally
sold and the money goes back to A: in both cases the capital owner
in A will get no more than he would have received if he had invested
the money in A. The situation is different when this capital owner
not only invests in B but also moves his place of living to B. He
earns, in monetary terms (using the exchange rate for comparison),
the same from his capital that he would have earned in A but faces
a lower price level; his real income increases.

It is obvious that this kind of personal movement need not be accompanied by capital flows: if the capital remains in A, the same benefit for its owner will result. Therefore, capital flows of the kind just indicated will be quite insignificant. The place of residence of nonworking (e.g., retired) capital owners will be affected, but that is of no interest in this context. The movement of such persons is today not, in fact, in the direction the foregoing analysis suggests: from countries with high border tax adjustments (EEC) to those with low adjustments (USA). This shows how minor this inducement resulting from the levy/subsidy system can be in the context of other forces.

Labor Movements

The real income of labor is equal in A and B. However, the income in monetary terms (always using the exchange rate as the means of comparison) is higher in A, in that A's price level is higher than that of B, and this can be exploited by a worker in the following way: if he works in A but spends his money in B, he will be better off than by earning his wage in B.

At first sight such an arrangement may seem impractical except for workers living near the border. But a worker may also live for many years in country A and either send money home to his family or return himself after a time and invest the saved money in B. This is what happens on a large scale in Europe today.

Conclusion

The impact of border tax adjustments on international capital flows is negligible. There is an inducement for a certain kind of labor movement. Given the low degree of international mobility of labor outside common markets, this influence is negligible as well.

PRELIMINARY CONCLUSIONS

The following conclusions are of a preliminary kind because only the results of the foregoing economic analysis are used. They will be complemented in Chapter 5 by legal considerations. Both points of view, the economic and the legal, have to be taken into account when the final conclusion (i.e., the answer to the basic question of this Part) is attempted.

The VAT and Other General Indirect Taxes

Neither the origin nor the destination principle interferes with maximum economic efficiency. The balance of payments is better protected from tax changes when the destination principle is implemented. Border adjustments at a rate lower than that of the domestic tax are not objectionable from the efficiency point of view but are not clearly preferable to the destination principle when the independence of the trade balance from domestic tax changes is considered. The destination principle should, therefore, be adopted.25 It will tend to lure away factors, especially labor, from their optimum location, but this effect is so minor that it can be neglected.

Selective Indirect Taxes

Optimum Trade Versus Maximization of Production

Earlier in this chapter the investigation of the compatibility of selective indirect taxes with the conditions for maximum economic efficiency led to the following result: if the origin principle is adopted, trade is optimized but production is not maximized. If the destination principle is followed, the reverse is true: maximization of production is achieved at the cost of optimum trade. What should be concluded from this result?

The only satisfactory solution would be the abolition of the selective domestic tax; there is definitely no other way to maximum economic efficiency. This radical way is barred, however, for the purpose of this study, in that the question to be answered is not what would be the optimum kind of domestic taxation, but how should domestic tax laws, whatever they may be, deal with internationally traded goods? In other words, the domestic tax law, insofar as it concerns goods not crossing international borders, is accepted as a fact. With this limitation of policy suggestions, the realm of the "second-best" is entered. If removal of the domestic tax which will always prevent the achievement of maximum efficiency is not possible, what would be the second-best solution to the problem?

This question can be tackled in three different ways. First, a decision between the two conflicting policies (optimum trade and maximized production) can be made on economic grounds, by attempting to prove that one is economically superior to the other. This is the way chosen by most of the economists who considered the question— e.g., Baldwin, Musgrave. Second, the same decision can be based on considerations of national tax sovereignty. Third, a compromise combining the two policies can be shown to have economic advantages over a clear choice.

Only the economic issues are taken up in the following sections. Chapter 5 will return to the problem and consider it from the viewpoint of national fiscal sovereignty.

A Compromise Solution

A selective indirect tax reduces the potential efficiency of the
world economy by more if either the origin principle or the destination
principle is purely implemented than if a compromise between the
two principles is adopted. It is preferable, therefore, to apply border
tax adjustments at a rate between zero and the full domestic tax rate.
The economic analysis necessary to prove this statement is of
some complexity. It is, therefore, omitted here and included in
Appendix I at the end of the book.

Is Maximization of Production Economically
More Desirable Than Optimization of Trade?

Most of the (few) economists who consider the choice between
these two principles for selective indirect taxes advocate adoption of
the destination principle for the reason that interference with the
maximization of production would do more harm to world efficiency
than failure to achieve the optimization of trade. The Tinbergen
Committee in Europe and economists Musgrave and Baldwin in the
United States are the main protagonists of this view. They do not
mention the possibility of combining the two conflicting policies but
seem to proceed from the assumption that a clear choice must be
made.

A Short-Term Consideration: Temporary Unemployment. In the
Tinbergen Report and in Musgrave's writings, the reason for favoring
the destination principle is barely indicated.[26] The notion is perhaps
that consumers can adjust more easily to changes than producers,
in that the prime effect of a selective indirect tax implementing the
origin principle is a decrease in production in the taxing country,
whereas under the destination principle mainly a decrease in consumption results (see Appendix I for a detailed analysis of these
effects). If production of the taxed good in the taxing country shrinks,
short-term unemployment will be the consequence. The more difficult
it is for other industries to absorb the released factors of production,
the greater is the harm caused by temporary unemployment. A shift
in consumption habits is not accompanied by such undesirable effects,
and dissatisfied consumers are likely to put less pressure on legislators
than unemployed workers.* It is doubtful, however, whether a

---

*A similar observation can be made in the case of dumping,
where the harmful effect on domestic production looms large in the
minds of legislators and government officials, whereas the positive
impact on those who consume the respective good is usually neglected.

temporary effect of this kind should carry much weight in the scales of economic policy. Long-term efficiency seems to be a goal that is superior to short-term considerations of this kind.

Baldwin, in contrast to other economists, gives specific reasons for his proposal to adopt the destination principle. The rest of this section will be devoted to a criticism of his views.

Robert E. Baldwin and the Viewpoint of "International Equity". Baldwin tries to solve the conflict between the origin principle and the destination principle for selective indirect taxes in the following way.27 He compares the effects of each principle on the economy of the taxing country with those on the rest of the world. Then he determines which principle distributes the inevitable adjustment burden in the most equitable way on these two economies. His result is that the origin principle will entail a heavy loss for the taxing country and a sizable advantage for the rest of the world, whereas under the destination principle the total burden is shared by all countries. Thus, he advocates adoption of the destination principle.

Even if Baldwin's basic premise, his view of optimal international distribution of adjustment burdens, is accepted, the validity of his conclusion must be disputed. His factual assumptions as well as his theoretical analysis cannot stand careful examination.

Baldwin assumes that foreign and domestic demand schedules for the product are inelastic, whereas domestic and foreign supply schedules are highly elastic. The elasticity of domestic supply is assumed to be about equal to that of supply in the rest of the world. The effects of the tax on production are described as follows. The origin principle will result in a significant decline in domestic production and a big increase in foreign production. Under the destination principle, the relatively small decline in total production will be shared by domestic and foreign producers. As to the effects on consumption, Baldwin says that the adjustment burden on consumers tends to be widely shared under either principle. He concludes, therefore, that the destination principle distributes the adjustment burden resulting from the tax in a more equitable way than the origin principle.

Baldwin clearly has in mind the traditional excise taxes (gasoline, cigarettes, liquor), inasmuch as demand for these products is relatively inelastic. However, as demonstrated earlier in this chapter, this small group of selective indirect taxes poses special problems in several respects. The enormously high rate of these excises alone makes any proposal to implement the origin principle a theoretical speculation; the domestic industry would very likely disappear if the origin principle were adopted. The fact that the raw material for these products is in the case of many countries almost exclusively imported means that the domestic tax could be replaced by tariffs. This fact suggests that the international problems of these excises should be dealt with under the heading of tariffs rather than under that of taxes. In any event, the two other groups of selective indirect taxes mentioned earlier in this chapter are at least of the same importance for international trade as the traditional excises. For these kinds of taxes, however, the assumption of inelastic demand is not correct. On the contrary, the demand for automobiles, furs, jewelry, record players, and television sets (to give but a few examples of typical selective indirect taxes) is of considerable elasticity. Baldwin's analysis is, therefore, not based on correct factual assumptions.

Baldwin's analysis of the distribution of the tax effects is correct with regard to the impact on production. Under the origin principle, domestic production will decrease and foreign production will increase (regardless of whether the respective good is imported or exported by the taxing country). Under the destination principle, both domestic and foreign production will decline (in the case of an imported good as well as in that of an exported commodity).

However, the effects on consumption are not correctly stated. Under the origin principle, consumption will decrease at home and abroad, inasmuch as the uniform world price of the good rises as a result of the tax. Under the destination principle, domestic consumption will decrease, whereas foreign consumption will increase. All this is, again, true for imported as well as exported goods. The figures drawn in Appendix I as well as those given by Baldwin[28] can be used to verify these results.

It is now obvious that there is a certain symmetry in the impact of the origin and destination principles on production and consumption. Under the origin principle, the effect on production in the taxing country is the opposite of that in the rest of the world, whereas the effect on consumption is parallel. Under the destination principle, in contrast, the effect on production is parallel, and the effect on consumption is opposite. This symmetry was overlooked by Baldwin who concluded that the burden on consumers will be "shared" by consumers in the taxing countries and in the rest of the world under either principle. He is right only with regard to the origin principle, and therefore his favoring of the destination principle seems to be unfounded.[29]

Result. With regard to selective indirect taxes, there is no convincing economic reason for favoring the destination principle over the origin principle.

Conclusion

Neither the origin principle nor the destination principle should be adopted for selective indirect taxes. Border tax adjustments of a rate between zero and the domestic tax rate should be applied. Individual treatment of each good in each country, taking into account the elasticities of supply and demand, would yield the best results from the economic point of view. Inasmuch as this approach, however, would be completely impracticable, a general rule seems to be preferable. A plausible, though arbitrary, proposal would be the following: exports and imports should bear 50 percent of the domestic tax.

Implementation of the pure destination (or origin) principle can be shown to be superior to this compromise only if certain general assumptions regarding demand and supply elasticities are made. However, in view of the large number of countries levying selective indirect taxes and the great variety of products involved, generalizations of this kind are bound to be incorrect.

Border adjustments for selected goods that exceed the rate of the domestic selective tax are harmful to economic efficiency in all but a few improbable cases.* Needless to say, border adjustments for selected goods on which there is no domestic tax at all, or only a general domestic tax, will also interfere with the conditions for maximum economic efficiency (see opening discussion of this chapter).

General Income Taxes

Border tax adjustments for general income taxes should not be introduced.

If border adjustments were introduced (on the basis of certain shifting assumptions), the sole justification for them seems to be the desire to keep the balance of payments independent of income tax increases or decreases, inasmuch as the pursuit of optimum efficiency does not require such adjustments. This has two major consequences.

1. The adjustments should be uniform for all internationally traded goods. Adjustments of this kind would be sufficient to neutralize the overall impact of the domestic tax increase (e.g., they would be sufficient to keep the balance of payments in equilibrium if the equilibrium existed previously). The uniformity would, on the other hand, be necessary in order to avoid violation of the conditions for

_____

*It may be repeated that maximum efficiency of the world economy is the policy goal. National gains resulting from either principle (terms of trade or economic growth advantage) are not considered. The balance of payments is also neglected, since selective taxes will only exert a minor influence on it.

maximum efficiency of the world economy (this can easily be seen
from the analysis at the beginning of this chapter).

2. Adjustments should be made only for tax changes, rather
than for the entire income taxes as they now exist. Introduction of
border tax adjustments designed to compensate for the whole domestic
income tax would not have the desired effect of protecting the balance
of payments from disequilibria induced by domestic taxes. It would
not serve to cancel out the effects of earlier domestic increases.
Since the first introduction and rise of income taxes, currency exchange
rates have been altered by almost every country in the world. Within
the last few years alone, almost all major trading nations changed
the par values of their currencies. Inasmuch as parity changes are
very often induced by disequilibria in the trade balances, it can safely
be said that most of the influences income taxes have had on international trade have been canceled out over the time by exchange
rate alterations. It would make no sense to attempt a second cancellation by means of introduction of border tax adjustments. A step
of this kind would have an effect contrary to the desired one: the
balances of payments of all countries would be heavily shaken, and
surpluses or deficits would come into existence or increase everywhere. Beneficial results would be a matter of coincidence. Therefore,
only adjustments for future changes should be made, if adjustments
were considered to be necessary at all.

This opinion is not in agreement with authorities such as
Musgrave and Baldwin. Varying rates of income tax border adjustments
for different products are envisaged by Baldwin[30] (even if he finally
does not advocate them because of his doubts about tax shifting), and
Musgrave seems to have in mind the same when he talks about the
"practical difficulties" of border adjustments for direct taxes.[31]
Musgrave indicates clearly that such border adjustments should
cover the whole domestic income tax (not only future tax changes),
the main reason why his "enthusiasm" for income tax adjustments is
"dampened" being the following: income taxes in Europe are not
much lower (if not higher) than those in the United States, so that the
latter would gain only very little from such adjustments.[32]

Selective Income Taxes

Particularly high income taxes that discourage the use of
productive factors in specific industries are considerably less
frequent than special income tax reductions designed to favor certain
industries. Only the latter kind of selective income taxation is
considered here.

A country imposing such a tax cannot, in the vast majority of cases, be expected to discourage exports of the favored industry or to subsidize imports of the respective goods; it would thereby partly or wholly defeat the purpose of the income tax reduction. Attention turns, therefore, to possible measures taken by other countries in order to reduce the negative effect of the selective tax on economic efficiency.

As in the case of selective indirect taxes, the policies leading to optimal trade and to maximization of production are conflicting. If free trade is not interfered with, a misallocation of the productive resources of the world will result, but consumers will enjoy optimum international trade. Interference with free trade, i.e., import duties and export subsidies applied by foreign countries in their trade with the taxing country, could remedy the misallocation of resources but would introduce new inefficiencies in that optimum trade would no longer prevail. How shall a foreign country decide the conflict in this case? Inasmuch as free trade may have a negative impact only on its production (not on its consumption) of the respective product, it should not interfere as long as its production is not seriously hurt. If the damage to its production is so great that it outweighs the benefit consumers enjoy from free trade, it should introduce import duties and export subsidies in order to counter that negative effect. Because comparison of production and consumption costs is difficult, if not impossible, the rule must be the following: a serious damage to production shall be the condition for application of border adjustments.

4

THE ECONOMIC ISSUES
IN THE BORDER TAX DEBATE:
AN ATTEMPT AT CLARIFICATION

The economic analysis of Chapter 3 was primarily designed to provide an answer to the following basic policy question: How should domestic tax laws deal with internationally traded goods? However, the results of this investigation can serve other purposes as well. First, they can be used as guidelines in the interpretation of the current international law of taxation of goods; Part III will show that economic considerations of this kind are indispensable means for the clarification of ambiguities in the pertinent GATT articles. Second, they can be applied in an attempt to deal with the different specific issues of the border tax debate. The great variety of the questions that have been raised in this context was demonstrated by Chapter 2. Inasmuch as most of these questions were not specifically considered in the economic analysis of Chapter 3, an attempt to provide answers to them is made in this chapter before resuming in Chapter 5 the investigation of the policy issue.

THE TAX SHIFTING CONTROVERSY
AND THE BORDER TAX PROBLEM

The heavy focusing on problems of tax shifting that characterizes most of the recent contributions to the subject of border taxes tends to cloud the real issues and to create misunderstandings and ambiguities. This does not mean that consideration of tax shifting is not very important for some aspects of the border adjustment problem. Consequently, these recent studies considerably enlightened the understanding of the effects of taxation on international trade and made very valuable contributions to the debate. If a thorough evaluation of the border tax issue is to be attempted, however, it is necessary to show clearly (1) the limitation of the significance of tax shifting for the problem of border tax adjustments, (2) the importance of distinguishing between different policies and different taxes—distinctions that are easily clouded if the problem of tax incidence is exaggerated—and (3) the danger of using a micro-economic approach, the approach to the border tax problem suggested by observations of tax shifting.

Chapter 3 demonstrated that the questions of maximum efficiency of the world economy and of equilibrium in the balance of payments have to be separated in a consideration of border tax adjustments. (A disequilibrium in the balance of payments can, of course, entail a reduction in potential economic efficiency, e.g., if it leads to severe unemployment in the deficit country and overemployment in the surplus nation, but efficiency losses of this kind are always tied to the peculiarities of the balance of payments.)

Tax Shifting and
Economic Efficiency

The Degree of Shifting and the Ideal
Rate of Border Adjustments

Chapter 3 demonstrated that, in the case of a selective indirect tax (e.g., an excise tax on automobiles), the destination principle will lead to the most efficient allocation of resources (at the cost of violating the condition for optimum trade). Many regard the best allocation of resources as the most desirable goal (Baldwin, Musgrave, the Tinbergen Committee). It would, however, be incorrect to assume that efficiency in resource allocation could be achieved even better if, instead of giving full tax rebates to exports and levying the entire amount of domestic tax on imports, the border adjustments would reflect the actual rate by which the tax is shifted forward in the domestic economy. Adjustments of this kind would, on the contrary, interfere with the international maximization of production.

In the case of general indirect taxes, Chapter 3 showed that border adjustments of any rate would be compatible with the achievement of maximum world efficiency. Again it would be incorrect to think that adjustments reflecting the degree of shifting could enhance efficiency even further.

Economic Efficiency and Different Kinds of Taxes

When full export rebates and import taxes are demanded in order to equalize for a domestic selective excise tax, the justification for this demand may be of an economic nature (favoring the maximization of production) or founded on considerations of national fiscal sovereignty (see Chapter 5). In any event, it would be easy for an observer who is not familiar with the justification to think that the reason for the border tax adjustments is the belief that the selective tax is fully reflected in the price of the product and the further belief that, for some reason (for instance, consideration of international competition) exports should be freed from the tax but imports should be subject to it. If he learns now from modern economists that income taxes are also shifted forward into the price, he sees no reason why border adjustments should not be applied to income taxes as well. Here we begin to sense the fallacy of the tax-shifting argument. Whereas economic as well as other reasons may suggest the destination principle for selective indirect taxes, the same reasons do not apply to income taxes. Focusing on the degree of tax shifting tends to blur this important distinction in that shifting may well occur to the same extent in both cases. If the phenomenon of shifting is regarded as the justification of border tax adjustments, the tendency is to treat all kinds of taxes alike, whereas considerations of economic efficiency and other factors suggest different treatment.

Tax Shifting and the
Balance of Payments

Domestic Tax Changes and the Trade Balance:
A Complex Relationship

In studies of border tax adjustments, the shifting issue is frequently introduced in a simplified form similar to the numerical example given in Chapter 2. (In Chapter 2, the example showed that full border adjustments and less than full shifting create an effect that looks similar to that of a tariff or a subsidy.) This may be sufficient to indicate the problem, but it is misleading in that it conceals the complexity of the relationship between domestic tax changes and the trade balance.

The simplest demonstration of the incidence of an indirect tax is provided by a model showing the supply and demand curves for a certain good. The tax shifts the supply curve upward, and the incidence depends upon the relative elasticities of supply and demand. If demand is very inelastic, the tax is shifted forward onto the consumer. If supply is inelastic, it is shifted backward onto the producer.[1] This model is useful for the micro-economic consideration of an indirect tax imposed on a certain selected good. In the case of a general indirect tax, the shift of the supply curve is only one of many economic developments following in the wake of the tax which influences prices. (For example, if the government spends

the new revenue on goods and services, a shift in the demand schedule
will occur, the extent of which depends on the government's relative
spending propensity.) Furthermore, in order to determine the impact
of the tax on international trade it is not sufficient to take account
of the immediate domestic price changes only.[2] The impact of the
tax on investment—depending on the money supply policy—and the
changes in real income that may result via the multiplier process
are of crucial importance for the trade balance. A reduction in real
income has a surplus-producing effect on the trade balance in that
it decreases the demand for imported goods. Determination of the
"incidence" of a general tax is not sufficient, therefore, to explain its
full impact on the trade balance—even if the incidence could be
exactly determined. This fact, which has often been overlooked, is
significant for the issue considered next.

Micro-economic Solution Versus Macro-economic Solution

The Micro-economic Approach to the Border Tax Problem. If "independence of the trade balance from domestic tax changes" (see Chapter
3) is accepted as a goal, it could be concluded that the best policy
would—at least in theory—be one that ensures that the prevailing
trade pattern remains entirely unchanged. Inasmuch as international
competition is a micro-economic phenomenon—different goods
compete on the world market, not different nations—it would seem
desirable to protect competition in each single product from any
influence exerted by any kind of domestic tax. This would completely
neutralize the impact of domestic tax changes on foreign trade. Tax
shifting, too, can be viewed as a micro-economic phenomenon, in
that the price effect of a tax change will never be uniform for all
goods involved. Thus, the best way to achieve the desired goal
appears to be the following: each domestic good should receive a tax
rebate exactly reflecting the tax incidence in its particular case, and
a corresponding import tax should be levied on each foreign good.
Many lawyers and economists have acknowledged that this would
in theory be the best solution to the border tax problem, although
practical difficulties seem to forbid its implementation.[3]

The Macro-economic Approach. The desired result—the independence
of the trade balance from domestic tax changes—can also be achieved
in another way. A general levy/subsidy system, applied at a uniform
rate, can be used in order to keep the ratio between total exports and
total imports unchanged. This could be called a "macro-economic"
solution to the tax problem. To be sure, the trade pattern prevailing
before the tax change would be altered in that the tax change affects

the prices of the various products to a different extent whereas the
border adjustments are uniform for all goods. But petrification of
the prevailing trade pattern is not a desirable goal in itself. Only
if the ratio between total exports and total imports changes and a
deficit or surplus in the balance of payments develops as consequence
is the economy of the taxing country threatened by possible adverse
effects. If trade patterns change but the balance of payments remains
in equilbrium, the impact on the taxing country is of a temporary
nature: after the economy has adjusted to the new pattern, no permanent
negative effect remains.

The observation that both solutions (micro-economic and macro-
economic) lead to the desired result with respect to the trade balance
does not suggest that one approach is superior to the other. But, as
Chapter 3 explained, every possible solution must also be judged from
the viewpoint of maximum efficiency of the world economy.

The Micro-economic Approach and Economic Efficiency. The analysis
of Chapter 3 has shown that border adjustments for a general tax
interfere with the conditions for economic efficiency if they are applied
at a different rate for different products. A micro-economic approach
to the balance of payments problem would, therefore, reduce potential
efficiency. Only a macro-economic approach, a general levy/subsidy
system, can achieve the two desired goals simultaneously: no violation
of the conditions for maximum efficiency, and independence of the
balance of payments from tax changes.

It would, therefore, be wrong to think that the best policy would
be one that leaves trade patterns entirely unchanged by a rise or
reduction in the domestic tax. The recognition of the fact that the
incidence of a general tax is different for each good suggests such
a product-by-product solution. But focusing on the tax-shifting
problem proves again to be misleading: this solution must be denounced
as one producing economic inefficiency. The idea that the effect of
a general tax could be completely restricted to the territory of the
taxing country by leaving the prevailing trade flows unchanged may be
appealing. However, economic efficiency requires that trade patterns
change and foreign economies adjust to the new situation created by
the tax. Other countries may not like this adjustment, but it is in
their own interest, in that petrification of certain trade patterns by
means of border adjustments with different rates weakens the world
economy.

Tax Shifting and Trade Effect of a Tax. There is still another flaw
in the micro-economic approach. The analysis above in "Domestic
Tax Changes and the Trade Balance: A Complex Relationship"
showed that exact neutralization of the price changes resulting from

a tax increase would not necessarily ensure that the ratio of exports and imports remained unchanged. An ideal system must take account of import reductions resulting from a fall in real income as well. In other words, the trade effect of a domestic tax change cannot entirely be explained by notions of tax shifting. Even if efficiency were neglected, therefore, a general levy/subsidy system might be superior to the product-by-product solution.

Efficiency Versus Balance of Payments Equilibrium? Governments, it seems, value a good balance of payments performance higher than the achievement of maximum world efficiency. Otherwise it could not be explained why, in order to prevent disequilibria, they resort to all sorts of measures economists unanimously denounce as breeding inefficiency: tariffs, quotas, export subsidies, nationalistic government purchasing policies. The avowed aim of the U.S. Trade Agreement Program was not a more efficient use of American resources but better access to export markets.[4] In the case of border adjustments for general taxes, however, no such unhappy choice between the two goals must be made: by adopting the macro-economic solution of a general levy/subsidy system and consciously disregarding the extent of tax shifting for various single products, economic efficiency and protection of the trade balance from disruptions can be achieved simultaneously.

"Trade Diversion" and "Trade Distortion"

Frequently the observation that the current border adjustments do not reflect the actual degree of shifting of indirect or direct taxes has led economists or lawyers to conclude that these adjustments have "trade-diverting" or "trade-distorting" effects. Ambiguous as these terms are, they imply, in any event, a negative value judgment: they suggest that something must be wrong with the adjustments. This is another example of the considerable lack of clarity that has accompanied the introduction of tax-shifting notions into the border tax debate.

Trade Diversion

In a paper submitted to the Joint Economic Committee's Subcommittee on Foreign Economic Policy, economist Helen Junz writes that the current border adjustments have "trade-diverting effects" in all the cases where the assumption of full forward shifting of indirect taxes is not true.[5] From the context it seems that she means effects that push the trade balance into a surplus or deficit.

However, the term "trade diversion" is used in economic literature usually in a narrow technical sense. Trade diversion, according to the common definition, takes place when goods from a more efficiently producing country are replaced by those of a less efficiently producing country because of some government interference such as discriminatory tariffs.[6] The key concepts of trade diversion and its opposite, trade creation, were introduced in 1953 by J. Viner in a study of customs unions.[7] Since that time, they have been a standard tool in the analysis not only of customs unions but also of other economic problems. For instance, they have been frequently evoked in the dispute about tariff preferences for less-developed countries, which—in the view of many experts—would lead to trade diversion.

Uniform border tax adjustments do not interfere with the conditions for maximum efficiency. Therefore, they cannot lead to replacement of low-cost production by high-cost production (see also "Fair International Competition" in this chapter). If they cause a surplus or deficit in the balance of payments they may give rise to a welfare loss, but the term "trade diversion" in its technical sense would not be appropriate to describe that loss. Moreover, a surplus-producing or deficit-producing effect does not necessarily mean that such a loss will occur at all (as explained in Chapter 3).

Therefore, it is incorrect (or at least misleading) to speak of a "trade-diverting" effect exerted by general border tax adjustments. Terms like "surplus-producing," "deficit-producing," or "change in trade patterns" would be more accurate.

Trade Distortion

The effect of border adjustments that do not reflect the actual degree of tax shifting has often been described as "trade distorting."[8] This term lacks a clear meaning. Changes in trade patterns, alterations in the overall trade balance, economic inefficiencies—each of these effects could be referred to. For this reason, the expression should not be used at all, or only after a definition has been given.

Even such a definition, however, may not completely do away with all ambiguities. For example, Robert Baldwin in his recent book Nontariff Distortions of International Trade defines a trade-distorting policy as any measure that causes internationally traded goods and services, or resources devoted to their production, to be allocated in such a way as to reduce potential world income.[9] Later in his book, Baldwin writes about the origin principle and the destination principle for general indirect taxes: "World production and trade . . . will not be distorted under either policy."[10] It seems that here a distortion of maximized production and a distortion of optimized trade are considered separately. This, of course, is not quite compatible with the earlier definition of "trade distortion," which referred to all of the conditions for maximum economic efficiency simultaneously. Thus it seems that even in such a carefully written book the term "trade distortion" has two meanings: a narrow one (violation of the condition for optimum trade) and a broader one (reduction of potential economic world efficiency).

The question of a common term for all interferences with international trade or division of production that reduce utopian world efficiency is hereby raised. "Tariffs" and "nontariff barriers to international trade" are still the most widely accepted concepts. Baldwin's suggestion "nontariff distortions of international trade" lets one think of changes in trade patterns (which do not necessarily lead to inefficiency) or of a violation of the condition for optimum trade (which is not necessarily the result of policies that otherwise create inefficiency; the origin principle for selective taxes is an example in point). Both of these implications are misleading. A more correct term probably must lack the desirable brevity: for example, "welfare-reducing interferences with international trade or the international division of labor."

FAIR INTERNATIONAL COMPETITION

The Businessman's View of Unfairness

It has been pointed out in Chapter 2 that businessmen, especially in the United States, tend to regard the current border tax adjustments as unfair. This view is based mainly on the empirical observation that, as a result of these adjustments, American firms can be undersold by European competitors even if their production costs (as reflected in the local price) are lower. A theoretical argument is also provided, contending that taxes should not be rebated on exports in that they are part of the genuine production cost, paid by the firm to the government in return for cost-reducing services.

Before the merits of these arguments are considered in detail, an attempt will be made to determine what businessmen commonly have in mind when they refer to "fair international competition," and whether their view of fairness makes sense from an economic point of view.

The Significance of the Businessman's Concept

To define and evaluate the businessman's concept of competitive fairness is of considerable importance, for two reasons:

1. Any government or legislature (in the United States or elsewhere) introducing or changing border tax adjustments will have to consider this concept in the preparation, implementation, and political defense of its action. This is vividly demonstrated in the United States by congressional hearings and debates as well as legal proceedings before the Tariff Commission in all matters of foreign trade policy, whether tariffs, nontariff barriers, or adjustment assistance are at stake.

2. Many government representatives and legislators who have to decide questions of foreign trade policy, if not the majority of them, tend to hold the same view in these matters as do businessmen, in that this appears to be a practical, sensible approach that appeals to common sense.

Basically, the opinion of the businessman seems to be that he should be given an equal chance with foreign producers, just as domestic firms—at least in principle—compete under conditions that are equal for everyone. Two specific demands can be discerned: the firm that is most "efficient" should be able to capture the market, and governments should not interfere with free international competition.

International Comparisons of Efficiency

If "efficiency" is understood as technological efficiency, the claim that the most efficient firm in the world should be able to undersell all the others must be rejected. David Ricardo's theory of "comparative advantage,"[11] which, in a simple classical model, explains why free international trade is beneficial for the countries involved, shows the flaw in that claim. What has to be "compared" in order to determine the "advantage" is not just the production of one particular good in two different countries—with the result that the country that is technologically more efficient in this production shall specialize in it; rather, the production of at least two goods in each country must be compared. If country A produces both a and b less efficiently than B but is, compared with B, even less efficient in a-production than in b-production, then both countries are better off if A specializes in b and B in a. To this basic insight, which has been unchallenged for two centuries, the competitive views of the businessman must yield.*

---

*The mechanism that allows the law of comparative advantage to work is the currency exchange rate between two trading countries, which is always so established that trade flows in both directions. Questions of comparative advantage are, therefore, determined partly by government activity, which is considered next.

Government Interference with Free
International Competition

The second claim of the businessman—that it is improper for governments to change the pattern of production and trade that would develop in a laissez-faire situation—cannot be easily dismissed. A case-by-case approach to the issue is necessary.

Two general observations can be made, one of an economic, the other of a legal nature:

1. If government activity influencing production or international trade is obviously of a selective kind or displays some other asymmetry, it is more likely to interfere with maximum efficiency than if it is general, nondiscriminatory, or symmetrical. A careful analysis, however, is always indispensable. For example, selective taxes are harmful, but general taxes are not. Taxing imports or subsidizing exports creates inefficiency (even if a uniform rate is applied), but a symmetrical treatment of exports and imports, a levy/subsidy system, does not (if minor factor movements are disregarded).

2. International regulation of economic activity of governments is faced with the necessity of applying relatively simple rules to relatively complex situations. As a consequence, only government interferences with production or trade that "clearly" and "seriously" jeopardize the efficiency of the world economy can be singled out and either prohibited or countervailed by actions of other governments. Activities the effect of which cannot be determined with reasonable clarity are necessarily outside the scope of international regulation. For example, if a country invests heavily in an excellent national educational system, it may thereby indirectly favor certain domestic industries over others. It is probably impossible to determine a specific violation of the conditions for maximum efficiency and to devise countermeasures to be applied by other countries.

Government interference with free international competition can consist either in an activity affecting the domestic economy without regard to international trade (production subsidies, minimum wage laws) or in measures particularly designed for internationally traded goods (tariffs, quotas, export subsidies, dumping). The businessman is especially suspicious of the latter kind of interference because it is most clearly visible: its consequence is that domestic prices in the respective countries (which may be assumed to reflect production costs) are no longer decisive for international competition. Having a lower domestic price than foreign competitors is no longer a guaranty for capturing the world market. Because comparisons of production costs loom large in the minds of businessmen, the following discussion will deal with this particular topic before the specific kinds of government interferences in the border tax case are considered separately.

International Cost Comparisons

It has been shown in Chapter 2 that the simplest and yet perhaps the most convincing way to challenge the current border tax adjustments is a comparison of production costs in the United States and the EEC. This is commonly done in the form of comparing domestic prices, in that they may be assumed, under competitive conditions, to mirror production costs. J. Frank Gaston and William J. J. Smith have established by careful empirical research[12] and government representatives of the United States have frequently pointed out that, for example, a French product may have a higher price in France than an American product in the United States, and yet it may be less expensive than the American product in all markets—in the EEC, in the United States, and in third countries. This is due to the border tax adjustments, not to differences in freight, insurance, or tariffs, as Gaston and Smith have shown. Does this not mean that a low-cost product is replaced in the world market by a high-cost product, as a result of artificial government interference with free competition?

It must be repeated that a "comparative advantage," which is decisive for the benefits resulting from free trade, cannot be established by comparing the production of one particular good in two countries. It is necessary to consider two or more goods and to determine in the production of which of them country A is comparatively more efficient or less inefficient than country B. This provides the answer to the intriguing question raised by a comparison of production costs. If the ratio of the production costs of all the goods produced in one country, the "productivity ranking," as it is sometimes called,[13] is decisive for the benefits of free trade, then it obviously does not destroy these benefits when all production costs of this country are artificially increased or decreased in the world market by the same rate. That does not alter the "productivity ranking" of the goods of this country.

This argument can be explained more thoroughly when the crucial role of the currency exchange rate is taken into account. International comparisons of production costs are possible only by means of an exchange rate: a parity change alters the ratio of the costs of producing a particular good in two countries, whereas the costs remain the same in absolute terms. The exchange rate determines at what point in the productivity ranking of all the goods of one country the break between exported products and import-competing products occurs. If border adjustments are introduced that make all of A's goods 15 percent less expensive in B and all of B's goods 15 percent more expensive in A, this breaking point will move: A will now begin to export some goods that were import-competing up to that time. This means that the "official" exchange rate no longer produces the comparison of production costs that is relevant for international trade. As far as international trade is concerned, A has depreciated its currency relative to that of B by 15 percent.*

On this basis, the comparison of production costs demonstrated by Gaston and Smith and many others must be reconsidered. The following example demonstrates the flaw in their argumentation. The industry producing good b in the United States is compared with the corresponding industry in France, a member country of the EEC. The official currency exchange rate is assumed to be $1 = 4 F** and France is assumed to have a VAT of 15 percent.*** The domestic price of the good is the same in both countries: $115 (460 F). In order to abstract from any existing difference in total tax burdens and isolate the effects of the border tax adjustments, it is assumed that costs and profits (both net of taxes) are also the same in both countries: $95 (380 F). In the United States, the price contains $20 income tax, whereas in France it contains $5 (20 F) income tax and $15 (60 F) VAT. Inasmuch as net costs and profits as well as taxes (prorated to each product) are exactly the same in the United States as in France, it should be expected that, transport costs and tariffs aside, neither country is able to undersell the other. However, the 15 percent border tax adjustments that implement the destination principle for France's VAT lead to another result. The French product will cost only $100 in the American market (in contrast to the $115 of the United States' product), whereas the American product is priced in France at 529 F ($115 + 15 percent) and cannot compete with the French product, which costs only 460 F.

How can it be explained and justified that the American product will disappear from all markets despite the fact that it is produced at the same cost as the French product? The answer begins with the recognition of the fact that production costs are actually not "the same"

---

*One must, however, be very careful with the statement that "the effect of an increase in border tax adjustments is similar to that of a devaluation." A change in border tax adjustments designed to implement the destination principle always accompanies a change in the domestic tax rate. The combined effect of these two changes on the trade balance is not that of a devaluation, as Chapter 3 has shown.

**The letter F stands for "French Franc." This does not, however, represent the current exchange rate between the dollar and the franc.

***This can be regarded as today's average rate in the EEC.

in the two countries. The 15 percent import charge and export rebate amount to a modification of the official currency exchange rate, with regard to international trade in goods. The exchange rate for this trade is not $1 = 4 F but $1 = 4.6 F. A good that costs $1 in the United States does not cost 4 F in France, but 4.6 F—and vice versa. Consequently, the American productions costs of $95 are not equal to 380 F (1:4) but to 437 F (1:4.6, or 1:4 + 15 percent). As far as this particular good is concerned, therefore, the United States happens to be a "high-cost country" and France a "low-cost country." It is unobjectionable in this case that buyers turn to the product of the latter.

By now it is obvious that uniform border tax adjustments amount to the institution of multiple exchange rates: international trade in goods (and partly trade in services as well) is subject to an "unofficial" exchange rate, whereas the official parity governs all other transactions (especially capital transfers). Multiple exchange rates are generally regarded as undesirable, and they are ruled out in principle by the International Monetary Fund.[14] But the term is commonly applied to currency schemes that distinguish between different goods.[15] Uniform border tax adjustments owe their important property of being compatible with the conditions for maximum efficiency to the very fact that they do not treat different goods in a different way. However, one price must be paid even for this special kind of multiple exchange rate scheme: it gives rise to factor movements that decrease the efficiency of the world economy. This effect could only be avoided if all countries were to apply the same rate of border adjustments.* Chapter 3 has shown, however, that welfare costs resulting from these factor movements are extremely small.

Government Interference I: Taxes

It has frequently been suggested that international trade should be freed from all domestic taxation, so that competition could not be distorted by differences in the tax systems of the various countries.[16] The opposite suggestion has also been made: no tax at all should be rebated on exports in that taxes are "location costs" similar to wages.[17] The realization that border tax adjustments work like a modification of the currency exchange rate, limited to international trade in goods, shows that neither of these opinions is correct. No

---

*This is envisaged for the EEC. It may be noted that in this respect introduction of a U.S. VAT would enhance world efficiency.

economic harm results (if equilibrium in the payments balance can be maintained) when parities are influenced by domestic tax levels just as they are influenced by wage levels, but the effect of taxes may as well be neutralized by border adjustments. The achievement of maximum economic efficiency is not conditioned upon either solution, as Chapter 3 has shown.

The fear that a country with low taxes may undersell a high-tax country in all commodities is as little justified as the fear that countries with low wages may completely undersell high-wage countries. A parity change—whether in the guise of border tax adjustments or not—would restore equilibrium in the balance of payments because most countries cannot afford a serious disequilibrium in the long run.

Government Interference II:
Activities That Reduce Business Costs

Government Services Provided to Business

Governments spend money out of the tax revenue to build and maintain roads and other public transportation systems, to provide fire and police protection, to establish facilities for the continuing education of workers, to finance postal, telephone, and telegraph services. All of these and many other government activities save the businessman money he would otherwise have had to spend in the production and distribution of his products. Were it not for these services, production costs would be higher. It is often claimed that taxes are, at least partly, payments to the government in return for these services. Therefore, it is concluded, rebating these taxes on exports is unfair, meaning that the pertinent services are provided free-of-cost to exporting firms (see Chapter 2).

It is true that government services of this kind introduce a difference between the marginal private cost of a product (the cost to the producer) and its marginal social cost (the cost to society of producing it), the latter being higher than the former. In the interest of economic efficiency, a tax making up for exactly this difference would be desirable; it would tend to equate prices with marginal social costs. In reality, domestic taxes are, of course, higher than this difference, and nothing can be done to remedy this situation. But should not an ideal solution be attempted for exports? If the destination principle is followed, should not just so much of the tax be rebated on exports that the remainder exactly reflects the difference between private and social costs that was introduced by the government services?

Before this question is answered, it is necessary to look at the import side, too. If imported goods do not benefit from corresponding services, a subsidy on imports is necessary in order to place them in exactly the same competitive position as domestic goods.[18] This would ensure that the difference between prices (net of tax) and social costs (seen from the viewpoint of the world community) was the same in the case of imported products as in that of domestic ones, so that domestic goods would not be preferred by consumers over foreign goods with the same social cost of production.* A comprehensive system adjusting for government services to business would, therefore, have to modify the destination principle: the export rebates as well as the import taxes would have to be somewhat lower than the domestic tax rate—e.g., 8 percent instead of 10 percent.

At this point the similarity of changes in border tax adjustments to exchange rate alterations proves again to be decisive. The switch from 10 percent border adjustments to those of 8 percent, which has just been described, would amount to a 2 percent appreciation of the taxing country's currency, restricted to the trade account. Apart from balance of payments considerations, efficiency is unaffected by such a change; it is neither enhanced nor reduced. (See analysis early in Chapter 3, where it was shown that border tax adjustments at a rate lower than that of the domestic tax do not interfere with the conditions for maximum economic efficiency.)

The situation is different when the wedge between social and private costs is not the same for all domestic industries. If a particular domestic industry receives more cost-reducing government services than all the other industries, uniform treatment of all exports and imports is no longer warranted. Chapter 3 has analyzed this case which is equivalent to a particularly low tax for one industry or any other specific subsidy.

The reality today is probably that government services are distributed to businesses in an uneven way. But it has already been pointed out that a main problem for international regulation of government activity is the degree of certainty with which economic phenomena can be observed. If it can clearly be established that cost-reducing government services favor a certain industry considerably more than others, international rules on subsidies apply (GATT Article XVI). But if this is not possible with a reasonable degree of certainty,

---

*Taxes are here disregarded because the destination principle ensures (for indirect taxes) that both imported and domestic products bear the same tax burden.

international economic regulation is powerless to remedy any economic inefficiencies that may result from government services.

The question of the magnitude of undetected inefficiencies of this kind remains open. It must be noted, however, that government services to business account only for a small part of the total tax revenue.19

Reductions in Factor Costs

Taxation or spending of tax revenue may reduce wages and profits. Usually, the reduction will be only a relative one, consisting in a retardation of increases that would otherwise have occurred. The general impact of taxation on the domestic economy can have this effect. It is also possible (as has been pointed out in Chapter 2) that government services provided to wage earners (e.g., low-cost housing) prove to be so extensive that demands for wage increases are less strong than they would be without these benefits. In this case it can be argued that, in effect, the government pays part of the wages. Regardless of the precise cause of the (relative) reduction in factor costs, foreign competitors will tend to regard the taxation or the spending of the tax revenue as an interference with free competition which puts them at a disadvantage.

As long as all sectors of the taxing country's economy are treated alike, no reduction of potential efficiency of the world economy results from government policies with an impact on wages. This can be concluded from the economic analysis of Chapter 3, where it was established that general taxation of labor income would not interfere with the conditions for economic efficiency, even if other incomes were not taxed. The concern of the foreign businessman is unjustified in that wage levels are always reflected in exchange rates. It has already been said that, for this reason, a country need not fear being undersold in all its commodities by low-wage nations. As in the foregoing case, government activity reducing the wages of workers in a certain industry only would amount to a subsidy, similar to a selective tax, and would have to be dealt with accordingly.

Government Interference III:
Implementation of the Destination Principle

Chapter 3 investigated the compatibility of the destination principle with maximum economic efficiency. What remains to be considered here is the frequent claim that application of the destination principle by the VAT countries is "protectionist" or "discriminatory."20

Protectionism

The difficulty of the question whether the current border tax adjustments have a protectionist effect results from the ambiguity of the word "protectionism." It can have either of two different meanings. First, it can refer to government action affecting internationally traded goods that leads to an increase in domestic production. Second, it can mean any government action that restricts imports. The answer to the question whether the destination principle for indirect taxes is a protectionist device depends, among other things, on the meaning given to the word protectionism. It is useful, in considering this question, to distinguish between selective and general indirect taxes.

If a selective indirect tax implementing the destination principle is introduced, the effect is that domestic production remains unchanged or (more likely) declines, whether the product is exported or imported by the domestic country (see "Preliminary Conclusions" of Chapter 3, and Appendix I). If by "protectionist" the level of domestic production is meant, the combined effect of the tax and the border adjustments is not, therefore, protectionist. (Changes in border adjustments are, as a rule, tied to tax rate changes, and it would be incorrect, therefore, to consider only one part of the government activity, namely the border adjustments, without regard to the concomitant tax increase.) If the product is imported by the taxing country, imports decline. In this sense, it is possible to speak of a protectionist effect.

If a general indirect tax is considered, the situation is considerably more complex in that the impact of the tax on the entire domestic economy has to be taken into account (see Chapter 3, "Increase of a General Indirect Tax"). If the government's spending propensity is the same as that of the private sector, both imports and domestic production will probably decline. It is then only possible to speak of "protectionism" if the second meaning (import restriction) is given to the word. If the government, however, spends all of the additional tax revenue (which may well happen), both imports and domestic production will probably increase. Now the word "protectionism" must be given the first meaning (increase in domestic production) if it is to be applied to this situation. It is, therefore, in any event incorrect to say that the destination principle for general indirect taxes has a "protectionist effect." Whatever meaning is given to the word, the statement can only be true when certain assumptions are made that are not more likely than others.

Discrimination

Border adjustments for a general indirect tax do not favor the goods of one country over those of another; they do not interfere with the most efficient international division of labor or with optimal international trade (see Chapter 3). Border adjustments for selective taxes that implement the destination principle solve the conflict between these two economic goals in favor of the first one, and the ambiguous term "discrimination" does not do justice to this complex economic problem. Only if imported goods are subject to a tax not levied on domestic products—i.e., if neither the origin principle nor the destination principle is adopted—is it correct to speak of discrimination against certain countries or against foreign products in general. Part III will return to this special case.

THE CONCEPT OF TAX NEUTRALITY

The preceding section on the "fairness" of international competition focused on the questions and arguments typically raised by businessmen in the border tax dispute. The remaining economic issues, now to be considered, center around the economic concept of "tax neutrality," another of the vague terms that are frequently used in the debate and which require clarification.

Domestic and International Neutrality

The concept of "tax neutrality" is of great significance for the domestic economy. For example, the question whether the turnover tax favors integrated industries, or whether the corporate income tax favors inefficient firms (which are quasi tax exempt), could be discussed under this heading. It is the international aspect of tax neutrality, however, that is of interest in the context of the border tax debate, and domestic problems are consequently now disregarded. It may be noted, however, that insofar as a switch from the cumulative turnover tax to the VAT increases economic efficiency within the respective country, the world community as a whole will be better off and the trading partners of the taxing country will, in the long run and to a different extent, benefit themselves from the change.

The term "international tax neutrality" can be understood in two different ways: it can mean neutrality with respect to the balance of payments or with respect to the most efficient allocation of resources and outputs.

Neutrality With Respect
to the Balance of Payments

If neutrality of this kind is favored, it is necessary to define the desired goal clearly: exact continuance of the pre-tax trade pattern, or simply preservation of the prevailing export/import ratio, regardless of whether or not the flow of particular commodities is changed. The analysis of this chapter thus far has shown that the first of these two goals is not only unnecessary but undesirable from the viewpoint of efficiency. With respect to the second goal, the destination principle for general indirect taxes will never achieve complete independence of the trade balance from tax rate changes, but it will approach this ideal result better than the origin principle or some compromise solution (see Chapter 3, "Tax Changes and the Balance of Payments").

Neutrality With Respect to International Trade and the International Division of Labor

Border Tax Adjustments: Hidden Tariffs and Export Subsidies?

It is undisputed in economic theory that tariffs as well as export subsidies reduce the efficiency of the world economy. In Chapter 2, it was mentioned that many writers, including eminent experts such as Kenneth Dam in the United States or Günter Schmölders in Europe, have expressed the view that the current border adjustments, at least insofar as they exceed the rate of actual tax shifting, create the same distorting effects on international trade as do tariffs or export subsidies. On the basis of the analysis of Chapter 3, this view must be rejected. Border adjustments for general taxes, unlike tariffs or subsidies, do not interfere with the conditions for maximum economic efficiency. The degree of tax shifting is irrelevant in this respect. It is true that import taxes alone, or tax rebates on exports alone, would have an effect equal to that of tariffs or export subsidies. But the fact that border tax adjustments treat exports and imports symmetrically makes them unobjectionable from the efficiency point of view. It is incorrect to separate the two aspects of border tax adjustments and investigate each of them as if the other did not exist.

Any statement that links border tax adjustments to tariffs can, therefore, be misleading. Two examples are offered:

1. It is often said (see Chapter 2, "The Government Representative's View: Changed Circumstances") that border tax adjustments are today more important as trade barriers than they were in the past because tariffs have been reduced so heavily during the last two decades. This statement suggests that border adjustments create the same inefficiencies as tariffs, and that now, after the first source of these inefficiencies is almost eliminated, attention must turn to the second. If it is acknowledged that border tax adjustments have effects different from those of tariffs, it is hard to see why their

relative "importance" for trade should depend upon the tariff level. They may perhaps change the trade balance between the taxing country and a certain other nation, but this is as undesirable for at least one of the two countries involved when tariffs are high as it is when they are low.

2. Helen Junz and others have suggested that international rules and multinational trade negotiators should treat changes in border tax adjustments similar to tariff changes.[21] This could lead to the unacceptable result that the trading partners of the taxing country respond to an increase in border tax adjustments, which creates no economic inefficiency, with tariff increases, which do create inefficiencies. Rather, one could think that changes in border tax adjustment rates should be dealt with in the same way as parity changes, i.e., they should be supervised by the International Monetary Fund. The question is, however, whether border tax adjustments are not tied so closely to domestic taxes that international organizations such as the GATT or IMF should not be allowed to influence them, just as they are not, for good reasons, empowered to dictate the internal tax policy of a member country. This important problem will be explored in Chapter 5.

Double Taxation

It has been said that adoption of the destination principle by one country and of the origin principle by another would interfere with "tax neutrality in international trade" and "distort trade relationships," in that goods imported by the former country from the latter would be "hampered by elements of double taxation."[22] The conclusion is that either all countries should adopt the destination principle or none of them should do so.

Insofar as this argumentation implies that "double taxation" of this kind would be economically harmful it must be refuted. From the economic point of view, border tax adjustments amount to a modification of the currency exchange rate (limited to trade), and therefore they do not lead to economic inefficiency. Just as two countries may change the exchange rate between their currencies, they may choose to adopt different tax principles for internationally traded goods; the economic effects are the same in both cases. The term "double taxation" is misleading in this context in that it implies that this tax treatment of international trade is economically somehow undesirable.

Whereas it is not necessary, from the economic viewpoint, that all countries adopt the same principle (origin or destination), it is indispensable that each country choose between the two principles. Analysis in Chapter 3 ("Border Tax Adjustments and Economic

Efficiency") has demonstrated that only the pure application of either principle or certain combinations do not interfere with the conditions for maximum efficiency, whereas most of the possible combinations violate one or more of these conditions. For example, a country adopting a VAT with no special treatment for international trade will subject imports as well as exports to the tax. This is economically inefficient and must be avoided.

The Most Efficient Use of World Resources

Latin American tax expert Reig has argued in favor of the destination principle because it "permits, from the producer's point of view, a better use of resources, the origin of raw materials, semi-finished goods, machinery . . . being irrelevant."[23] The underlying reasoning seems to be that the producer should buy inputs where they are "really" the least expensive, without regard to taxes. Chapter 3 has shown for general indirect taxes that economic inefficiency can be avoided only if domestically produced inputs are not taxed and if a country adopting the origin principle taxes all exports, whether they are intermediate or final goods, at the same rate. Reig's argument is, therefore, with regard to general taxes, not convincing.[24] The taxation of the input in the origin country must be regarded as a modification in the exchange rate and thus does not interfere with the most efficient use of world resources.

Neutrality With Respect to International Factor Movements

The destination principle is not "neutral" in this respect (see Chapter 3, "Indirect Taxation and International Factor Movements"). Factor movements detrimental to economic efficiency could only be avoided if all countries would implement border tax adjustments of the same rate. (This furnishes a new reason why adoption of a VAT by the United States would be desirable.) The differential between the existing rates is, however, even today not as large as it may superficially seem. Retail sales taxes, which cover imported goods but not exports, have exactly the same effect with regard to possible factor movements as adjustments for domestic taxes at the border. When, for example, a Japanese television set is imported into the United States and sold in New York City, a sales tax of 7 percent is imposed on it. The economic effect would have been the same if a 7 percent import tax had been levied at the border in order to equalize for the tax on domestically produced sets. The typical result of the destination principle, namely that all final prices in the taxing country are higher by the percentage of the tax than in a country without taxes (transport costs and tariffs disregarded) does not depend upon the technicalities of the taxation. The rate differential between New York City and, for example, West Germany (with its 11 percent VAT) is thus only 4 percent.25

5

BORDER TAX ADJUSTMENTS
AND NATIONAL TAX SOVEREIGNTY

This chapter resumes the consideration begun in Chapter 3: How should domestic tax laws deal with internationally traded goods? Although economic issues will again be prominent, the focus of this chapter is entirely different from that of the two preceding chapters. Up to now, the utopian goals of maximum economic efficiency and equilibrium in all payments balances provided the touchstone for judging the various answers to the question posed above. This chapter, in contrast, will focus on the power of the state to levy taxes. This fiscal power, a part of the very foundations on which each state is built, is a legal phenomenon, deriving from constitutional law, and can therefore not be judged entirely in terms of utopian economic goals.

The first two sections of this chapter will deal with the following questions: Is it desirable, or even necessary, that the power of a state to tax internationally traded goods be limited by international regulation? If the answer is affirmative, and if several alternative limitations are equally sensible from the international viewpoint, which of these limitations represents the least interference with the national fiscal power? There will follow an investigation of how the state's tax power with respect to internal trade is limited in two important federations, one existent and one emerging: the United States of America and the United States of Western Europe. Conclusions can be drawn for the most sensible international limitation of fiscal sovereignty. The chapter closing points out the consequences that the link between border tax adjustments and the legal power of the state to levy taxes has for an ideal law of taxation of internationally traded goods.

SHOULD INTERNATIONAL LAW LIMIT THE TAX POWER OF THE STATE WITH RESPECT TO INTERNATIONALLY TRADED GOODS?

Conflict Between the Fiscal Sovereignty of Different States

Taxation of Foreign Consumers

The following argument is frequently made against application of the origin principle for indirect taxes: if the taxing country does not relieve exported products from taxes, the consumers of these goods will in effect pay the tax and thus contribute to a state budget from which they themselves do not receive any benefits.[1] All supporters of this argument believe that it is only valid insofar as the tax is shifted forward to the purchaser. However, it is here suggested that the question raised by this "consumer benefit doctrine" does not depend upon the extent of tax shifting. Even if the price of an exported good is not raised as a result of the introduction or increase of a tax, the fact remains that the producer of the good pays taxes and that he pays them out of the price he receives from the foreign purchaser. The hypothetical question of what the final price would be if there were no tax does not alter the fact that a part of the money the foreign consumer pays for the good ends up in the treasury of the exporting state. He therefore indirectly contributes to the budget of a foreign state by buying the latter's product. The taxes the exporting country receives from exporters are paid by them out of the revenue of their export sales, and these taxes help the country to finance its government expenditures, whether the taxes are shifted forward into the price or not.

The Nature of the Conflict

It could now be argued that, as a matter of sovereignty, each state has the exclusive right to tax its citizens or residents and that no other state should interfere with that right. Consequently, no state should extend its taxation, not even indirectly, to nationals and residents of foreign states who do not own property or carry on business within its borders. This would mean that the destination principle should be applied to exports in respect of all taxes.

On the other hand, however, an argument could be made that the importing nation, insofar as it allows goods to be imported, renounces its sole right to tax its consumers and leaves it to the exporting country whether or not it levies taxes on these goods.

Obviously, a formalistic argument is here rebutted by a no less formalistic one, and this exchange of arguments does not touch the core of the matter. It is worthwhile to investigate the true reason why a state should not indirectly extract taxes from consumers of another nation, apart from formal considerations of sovereignty. The basic foundation for this view seems to be a certain concept of the nature of taxation, one that links the payment of taxes to the benefits received in return from government. Two aspects of the problem can be distinguished.

The "Positive" Aspect. The tax revenue extracted in an indirect way (through exports) from foreigners is spent on services to the citizens of the origin country. It is claimed that no state should finance benefits to its nationals by means of taxes imposed indirectly on foreigners. This claim rests on a distinction between government expenditures and private expenditures that will not stand close analysis. First, it must be noted that any money paid for an imported product benefits the citizens of the origin country, whether it ends up in the treasury or in a private man's pocket—in the form of wages, profits, interest, etc. It does not matter whether the expenditures financed out of the export revenue are private or public because in any event the citizens of the origin country, not those of the destination country, reap the benefits. Second, the different degrees of socialization observed among today's trading nations must be considered. Endeavors that in one country are financed from tax revenue may in other countries be paid for by private persons (i.e., transportation systems, education, health services, art, mass media).

It could, of course, be argued that in the case of a tax it is the foreign government that forces the purchaser to contribute to the welfare of the origin country whereas otherwise it is the private businessman, and that only the former is undesirable. However, this argument is shaky because prices net of taxes are heavily influenced by kinds of government activity other than taxation. Domestic employment and inflation policies or the fixing of the currency exchange rate may serve as examples. The conclusion is, therefore, that a purchaser who wishes to avoid contributing to the well-being of the citizens of a foreign country cannot look to the destination principle to serve his purpose. He will have to boycott the products of that country altogether.

The "Negative" Aspect. The purchaser of the export commodity, it is said, "gets nothing in return" for his (indirect) payment to the foreign exchequer. It is claimed that no tax should be (indirectly) extracted from him in that case: "No taxation without benefaction." This claim

must be refuted. A purchaser who buys a good imported into his
country votes with his money for this particular product. He cannot
complain that he gets "nothing in return"; he gets the imported good.
He himself has decided that this good is worth his money.

Conclusion

The concept of tax sovereignty does not mean that a state should
be given the exclusive power to impose taxes, in a direct or indirect
way, on its citizens. The national tax power remains untouched if
consumers buy imported products the price of which contains taxes
of foreign countries; the power of the state to tax its citizens at will
is thereby not limited. Therefore, the apparent conflicts between the
tax sovereignty of different nations are no reason for international
law to limit the power of the states to tax internationally traded goods.

Conflict Between the Tax Power of a State and
the Economic Interests of Other States

Short-Term Economic Adjustments

It is theoretically possible for a state to limit the impact of its
tax policy entirely to its territory. This could be done by a complicated, elaborate scheme of different levies and subsidies on all
internationally traded goods. Superficially this may seem to be the
most desirable goal, because no other country would be burdened with
short-term adjustments of consumption and production, causing hard-
ship to some businessmen and temporary unemployment. However,
Chapters 3 and 4 have shown that schemes of this kind create economic inefficiency. In the long run, accumulated inefficiencies would
certainly outweigh the advantage of sparing economic adjustments.
Therefore, international regulation should not try to prevent countries
from passing on adjustment burdens to other nations.

Long-Term Economic Efficiency

A country can use its tax power with respect to internationally
traded goods in a way that tends to reduce the possible efficiency of
the world economy. This would happen, for example, if a state subjects
both its imports and its exports to a general indirect tax (see Chapter
3). All countries would benefit if international regulation restricted
the tax power of states so that it could not be used in a way that would
result in economic inefficiency—just as all trading countries that are
members of GATT benefit from the restriction of the state's power

to interfere with free trade by imposition of tariffs, quotas, or multiple exchange rates. Chapter 3 demonstrated the kind of restriction necessary to achieve this purpose.

However, Chapter 3 also showed that the origin principle and the destination principle are equivalent from the pure efficiency point of view, for all kinds of taxes. The considerations that suggest, in the economic interest of all countries, adoption of the destination principle for general indirect taxes and a medium adjustment for selective indirect taxes are rather vague in that economic realities elude clear-cut solutions in this respect. It may well be that either the destination or the origin principle or a medium adjustment means a very severe infringement of national tax power. If this were so, this consideration might override those somewhat vague economic factors, and the conflict between national tax sovereignty and the economic interests of other countries may have to be resolved in favor of the former. The following section therefore investigates which principle is most compatible with the fiscal sovereignty of states. The underlying assumption is that countries must choose between the origin principle and the destination principle (or apply some inter- mediate adjustments); taxation of both exports and imports is clearly inferior to either principle from the viewpoint of long-run efficiency.*

DESTINATION PRINCIPLE VERSUS ORIGIN PRINCIPLE: WHICH INTERFERES LESS WITH NATIONAL TAX SOVEREIGNTY?

Raising of Revenue by Means of Selective Indirect Taxes

If a country's trade balance is in equilibrium, it does not matter for revenue purposes whether it taxes all exports (origin principle) or all imports (destination principle) provided that the tax rate applied in each case is the same (e.g., 15 percent). The situation is different when a country chooses to raise revenue by means of a selective tax.

---

*See Chapter 3 (for general taxes). In the case of selective taxes on one particular product only, taxation of both exports and imports at one time is not possible in the strict economic model in that this commodity will either be exported or imported by the taxing country. If economic reality shows that this is not the case, the analysis of a tax on several goods applies.

The traditional excise on liquor is a case in point. In most countries it is a pure revenue tax without a genuine social purpose (a moral judgment against liquor will usually be only an excuse for the tax, not the reason for its imposition). If a country is a net importer of liquor, i.e., if it consumes more liquor than it produces, taxation of consumption (destination principle) provides a larger tax base than taxation of production (origin principle) and therefore serves the fiscal purpose better. If, on the other hand, a country is a net exporter of liquor, taxation of production seems to be preferable. However, if the selective tax is increased by so much that it reduces to zero the price difference between the domestic product and the least expensive foreign equivalent, consumers will turn to the latter, and the tax base will be eroded. Inasmuch as international price differences are seldom of extreme dimensions and domestic supply tends to be rather elastic in the long run for all products, taxation of production (origin principle) would, in most countries, have to be limited to a modest rate. Taxation of consumption, on the other hand, can (if demand is sufficiently inelastic) be increased up to a very high percentage without destroying the respective domestic industry. High taxation of consumption will raise more revenue than low taxation of production unless exports exceed domestic consumption by a very large amount, which will be a rare case.*

Thus, in both cases—whether the country is a net exporter or a net importer before the tax is imposed—the destination principle generally provides for the largest tax base possible. Only the elasticity of domestic demand limits the state's ability to raise revenue—and usually the goods picked for revenue excises are characterized by extremely inelastic demand. The origin principle is generally inferior for revenue purposes in both cases. It makes it impossible for the state to exhaust a revenue excise up to the limit of demand elasticity. To oblige a country to adopt the origin principle for selective indirect taxes means, therefore, a much more serious limitation of its power and ability to raise revenue than to force it to implement the destination principle. Even a "medium" border adjustment (e.g., 5 percent import tax in the case of a 10 percent domestic tax) would erode the broadest possible tax base; the effect would be similar to that of the origin principle—consumers would try to evade the tax by purchasing imported goods.

---

*Such cases do occur, however. The oil-producing countries of the Middle East provide a notable example. Especially if the exporting country has a monopoly power in the international market, taxation of exports may be preferable for revenue purposes.

Taxation as an Instrument of National Policy

The Purposes of Taxation

Modern theory of public finance is not concerned with the question that troubled economists in the past—whether or not the state should use taxation for other than purely fiscal purposes. The classical theorem that a tax should be motivated only by fiscal considerations, and that it should be "neutral" in its effects on the economy, is no longer accepted. The other extreme, the opinion that the primary if not sole purpose of taxation is the achievement of economic effects such as price stability, is equally rejected. Economists generally agree today that tax policy has to pursue, and combine harmoniously, two equally important goals: the raising of revenue, and the achievement of desired social and economic effects.[2]

Taxation as an Instrument of Social Policy

Taxation can serve social purposes mainly by interfering in a regulatory manner with the distribution of income and wealth. Furthermore, it can restrict socially undesirable, or promote socially desirable, consumption or production. The ways in which these goals can be pursued differ greatly with the kind of the tax involved.*

Indirect Taxation. In the case of indirect taxes, redistribution of income and wealth can be achieved by two different means:
1. Certain persons can be relieved from indirect taxes. As a practical matter, this can usually be done only by the government refunding taxes to these persons or permitting them to deduct indirect taxes paid on purchases from direct tax liability. In effect, the favored persons pay less than other people either for all goods (general tax) or for certain commodities (special tax), and thereby the desired social result is achieved.

If, in this situation, imported products are not taxed (origin principle), the desired distinction between different people cannot be made in this respect. The more imported goods consumers buy, the

---

*Indirect taxes and income taxes are the only kinds of taxation considered here despite the fact that other taxes (e.g., estate and gift taxes, property taxes) may serve important social functions as well. The reason is that these latter taxes have no (or only little) impact on international trade in goods. Border tax adjustments have never been suggested for them.

more is the desired social purpose defeated. Only the destination principle allows unlimited pursuance of a social policy that consists in making all goods less expensive for certain citizens by means of indirect taxation.

2. Different tax rates can be applied to different products. This is the path chosen by almost all countries that levy indirect taxes. Selective taxes on luxury goods serve a social purpose because they fall more on wealthy citizens than on the poor. By lowering the tax rate for necessities such as food and clothing and increasing it for luxuries such as television sets, jewelry, and automobiles, the regressive character of a general indirect tax can be considerably mitigated, and it may even be turned into a mildly progressive tax.*

Distinction between different goods enables a state to pursue other social purposes in addition to regulation of the distribution of wealth. The distribution of goods that are dangerous for society (private guns)** or which impose special burdens on it (automobiles and other pollutants) can effectively be restricted by levying an indirect tax on them.

It is obvious that selective taxation can achieve these socially desired results only if imports are taxed as well. A particularly high tax on jewelry does not hurt the wealthy citizen much if he can buy foreign jewels without paying the tax. Whereas the price for the imported commodity may be higher than the price net of tax of the domestic product, it may well be much lower than the latter's gross price. Similarly, a tax on guns would all but fail to restrict private purchases if it could be evaded by buying guns from abroad. A tax on pollution-prone cars would not alleviate a country's pollution problems if the same cars could be imported free of tax.

Thus, whichever way a country chooses to apply indirect taxation as an instrument of social policy, it will fully achieve the desired goals only if it adopts the destination principle.

Income Taxation. Income taxes are important means of social policy because they can be adapted very flexibly to many purposes. In the

---

*A tax is called regressive when it takes a larger fraction from low incomes than it does from high, and it is called progressive when it does the reverse.

**Today, cigarettes can also be included in this category in that recent research has proved that health hazards result from cigarette smoking. Many countries put high taxes on cigarettes, or on tobacco in general.

context of taxation of internationally traded goods, only the income tax on businesses is of interest. It can be transformed into a powerful instrument for the redistribution of income and wealth if the tax rates are made progressive. Almost all Western countries attempt to do this. A policy consequently directed toward this goal can only be successful if all corporations and unincorporated businessmen are subject to the tax. If a firm that produces and distributes exclusively export products is exempted from income taxation (destination principle), a loophole is opened for tax evasion, and the desired social justice cannot be achieved.

An income tax on business may serve other social purposes as well. A corporation that is socially undesirable—e.g., with a plant that puts a heavy pollution burden on society—could be subjected to a particularly high profits tax in order to force it to gradually cease production or at least to stop further expansion. Conversely, in a region with high unemployment new industry could be attracted for social reasons by a particularly low profits tax.* In both cases, exemption of export production from the special tax measure (destination principle) would partly defeat the social purpose.

Result. Social purposes, especially a socially desired distribution of income and wealth, can be effectively pursued by means of taxation only if the destination principle is implemented for indirect taxes and the origin principle is applied to income taxes.

Taxation as an Instrument of Economic Policy

The economy of a country can be controlled and influenced by means of tax policy, especially in order to approach the important goals of stability, full employment, and growth.** The United States gradually began to employ taxation for this purpose in the 1930s and 1940s, when the "new economics" taught by John Maynard Keynes was increasingly adopted by scholars and politicians. A landmark on the way to a new, active fiscal policy was the Employment Act of

---

*An effect of this kind could also be achieved, at least in theory, by means of indirect taxation. However, the use of income taxation for this purpose creates far less practical difficulty.

**The spending of the tax revenue may be an even more powerful instrument of economic policy than the taxation itself. It is neglected in the following consideration because it is independent from the tax principles applied to international trade.

1946 which created the Joint Economic Committee, instituted the President's Council of Economic Advisors, and obliged the President to present to Congress an annual economic report.

Whereas neither the destination principle nor the origin principle in itself necessarily favors stability or growth, apart from its impact on the balance of payments,* the success of domestic tax policy directed toward these goals may well depend upon which principle is adopted for international trade.

The development of a country's economy is decisively affected by consumption and investment. The main function of taxation as an instrument of economic policy is, therefore, to increase or decrease either of these two factors. The impact of taxation on the propensity to consume and the propensity to invest is extremely complex, but a few simple observations regarding the taxation of internationally traded goods can be made.

If a decrease in consumption is mandated in order to achieve the desired economic goals, both indirect and direct taxation can be employed for this purpose. Raising indirect taxes by itself leads to a decrease in private consumption, but only if imports are taxed as well (destination principle). Otherwise, consumers will simply turn to imported goods, and although the ratio between consumption and saving remains about the same, a deficit pressure is exerted on the trade balance. Raising the income tax for smaller incomes can also dampen consumption. In this case, income earned from export sales should not be exempted. The reasoning is similar in the reverse situation, i.e., if consumption is considered to be too low.

If tax policy focuses on influencing investment, the income tax on business appears to be the most effective instrument. Incentives or disincentives for investment can be provided by income tax laws in various forms. Application of the destination principle would mean that one sector of the economy, the export industry, could not be affected by income tax measures. In countries with a high ratio between exports and national product, this would severely restrict the impact of income tax policy.

---

*Border tax adjustments for selective taxes can be employed in order to achieve growth in a certain country at the cost of other countries by heavily protecting or subsidizing particular industries. This, however, is the very national policy that international regulation of economic activity should seek to restrict. The statement in the text must be read with the qualification in mind that a purely national point of view is not being taken but that the common interests of the international trading community are being pursued.

Thus, economic growth, price stability, and full employment
can be achieved more effectively by national tax policy if the destination principle is adopted for indirect and the origin principle for direct
taxation. The reason is that only these principles permit tax policy
to affect total domestic consumption and all domestic incomes.

A Practical Example: Italy in August 1970

In August 1970, a new government took over in Italy after a long
period of political and economic instability.[3] It found itself faced
with high inflation, a strong deficit pressure on the balance of payments
lagging production, and, above all, an enormous need for state revenue
in order to implement desperately needed social reforms. In the
subsequent weeks, the new government took various measures in order
to raise more revenue and shift resources from consumption to investment. The main step was a sharp increase in various selective indirect taxes. Italy's gasoline suddenly became by far the most expensive in Western Europe. Television sets, cameras, records and
record players, certain alcoholic beverages, perfumes, gold jewelry,
antiques, cosmetic articles, playing cards, and a variety of other
luxury goods were subjected to special sales taxes. This provided
the government with additional tax revenue, dampened consumption,
and reduced imports. The selection of the taxed goods was obviously
motivated by social considerations. Thus, all the main purposes of
taxation—revenue, social policy, economic regulation—were pursued
simultaneously by a single tax measure. This was supplemented by
changes in the income tax law designed to spur investment. It is
obvious that the selective indirect taxes would have been less effective
in all respects if imports had not been taxed as well. Similarly, the
investment incentives would have had a more limited effect if they
had been restricted to production designed for domestic consumption.

TAXATION OF INTERNAL TRADE IN FEDERATIONS: MODEL SOLUTIONS FOR WORLD TRADE?

Taxation of Interstate Commerce in the United States

Restriction of the States' Tax Power

The tax power of GATT member countries is restricted with
regard to taxation of internationally traded goods by the pertinent

GATT rules. Any future rules, implementing an ideal solution, would also have to impose limitations on national tax sovereignty. Similarly, the Constitution of the United States restricts the tax power of the fifty states with regard to taxation of goods traded between them; Article 1, Section 8, clause 3—the "commerce clause"—contains this limitation.

This section will deal with but one of the many conflicts between the commerce clause and the states' tax power and will show how this conflict was solved by the individual states, the Federal Congress, and the Supreme Court of the United States. The role the fiscal power of the states played in this conflict will give some valuable indications for a solution of similar problems on the international level.

State Sales Taxation and the Destination Principle

It was the Depression which inspired the first widespread use of retail sales taxes in the United States (see Chapter 1). By 1937, a total of 31 states* had enacted general sales tax laws.[4] Today, not only the vast majority of the 50 states apply sales taxes, but, in addition, many municipalities do the same. Almost all of these taxes are levied at the retail stage. The rate of sales taxation (state and local tax combined) varies greatly within the United States.

Soon after the introduction of the first state sales tax, a problem arose that has plagued many states and cities up to the present time: consumers tried to evade the tax by purchasing goods from other states. To be sure, evasion was not accomplished if goods manufactured in other states were imported into the taxing state and sold there by a retailer. (Illegal evasion is not considered here.) But consumers could visit a neighbor state with a lower (or zero) sales tax and purchase as many goods as they could transport back. The commerce clause generally prohibits levying of duties on imports from another state, even in the form of a tax, so that the taxing state could not act like a sovereign country and tax these imports. Far more significant, however, was the possibility of ordering goods from a mail-order house located in a state with a lower sales tax or no sales tax at all. Again the commerce clause makes it impossible for a state to levy duties, equivalent to its sales tax, on these imports.[5]

---

*In this section on "Taxation of Interstate Commerce in the United States," the term "state" refers to one of the fifty states (not to other nations), and the terms "exports" and "imports" refer to trade between the sister states (not to international trade).

These two means of evading the tax without recourse to illegality meant that the destination principle, which superficially seems to be a natural consequence of a retail sales tax, was not fully implemented for sales taxation. Not all final goods imported into the taxing state were subject to the sales tax but only those distributed by a retailer in that state. Those goods imported directly by the consumer were partly subject to the origin principle (in the case that the consumer bought them in person in another state) and partly exempt from any sales taxation at all (in the case of mail orders from another state: under the commerce clause, the mail-order house is not permitted to include the sales tax of the state in which it is located in the price charged to a customer residing in another state).

It was shown earlier that full implementation of the destination principle for indirect taxes is required if a state effectively wants to achieve the aims of taxation. In the context of interstate commerce in the United States, the purely fiscal purpose of taxation—the raising of revenue--is dominant among these aims. Because in the early 1930s, introduction of a sales tax in a state meant that the destination principle was only partially implemented, the states were not able to employ indirect taxation as a means of raising revenue as effectively as they could have without the restrictions imposed on them by the commerce clause. Direct imports, especially those effected through mail orders (which could be anticipated to develop into a highly significant and frequent kind of transaction), constituted a severe drain upon potential state revenues. This clash between the fiscal interests of the states and the liberation of interstate trade prescribed by the commerce clause was resolved in 1937 by a decision of the Supreme Court of the United States.

Full Implementation of the Destination Principle
by Means of the Use Tax

The states that introduced sales taxation soon discovered how they could circumvent the commerce clause and extend indirect taxation to goods directly imported by consumers. They could tax the "use" of all goods within their territory and exclude the use of articles already subject to their sales tax. In effect, such a use tax was applied only to goods directly imported by consumers. A tax law of this kind, supplementing the state sales tax with a use tax, was enacted in the State of Washington in the early 1930s. The statute was assailed as a violation of the commerce clause but was declared constitutionally valid by the Supreme Court of the United States.[6]

The opinion, written by Justice Benjamin Cardozo, is characterized by rather formal reasoning. Cardozo realized, of course, the purpose behind the tax scheme. But he did not interpret the commerce clause from an economic point of view, although it is at least conceivable that the clause was designed to ensure the economic benefits of free interstate trade. If he had done so, he would probably have concluded that the use tax achieved economically the same effect, in an indirect way, that the states were prohibited—by the accepted construction of the commerce clause—from achieving in a direct way by imposing an import tax. But significantly, Cardozo chose to base his conclusions not on notions of economic efficiency but on a broad concept of the state's tax power. He pointed out that a state is at liberty to tax all aspects of ownership, separately or cumulatively, and that "use" is one of these aspects. As long as the tax was not levied directly on the import transaction but on some activity following the importation, it did not violate the commerce clause, Cardozo argued, even if the motive behind it was clearly the same as that behind an import tax.

The consequence of this Supreme Court judgment was easy to anticipate: most states supplemented their sales tax by a use tax, thus fully implementing the destination principle.

The Continued Fight of the States for the Destination Principle

The clash between the fiscal power of the state and the commerce clause had been decided in favor of the former. But that did not mean that the revenue drain resulting from direct imports was in fact stopped. The practical difficulties encountered in enforcing the use tax laws were tremendous. Several methods have since been used to achieve complete implementation of the destination principle.

One method consists of state statutes requiring nonresident firms (especially mail-order houses) to collect the tax from purchasers in the taxing state. This means, e.g., that the State of New York utilizes the seller who resides in the State of Massachusetts as an agent for collecting the New York use tax from purchasers residing in New York. Again, the Supreme Court of the United States decided in favor of the fiscal power of the state and held that a statute of this kind did not, under certain circumstances, violate the commerce clause.[7]

Another possible way is demonstrated by the Jenkins Act (State Cigarette Taxes).[8] The purpose of this federal statute is to assist states in the full implementation of the destination principle with respect to cigarette taxes. These taxes, belonging to the small group of traditional excises, are a significant source of revenue in many states. The Act applies to all persons (legal or natural) who sell cigarettes in interstate commerce and ship them directly to consumers residing in a state taxing the sale or use of cigarettes. It requires these persons to file each month a statement with the tobacco tax administrator(s) of the state(s) into which shipment is made containing the names and addresses of all customers in that state and the quantity and brand purchased by each customer during the previous month.[9] In this way, collection of a use tax on cigarettes is greatly facilitated and states can effectively apply the destination principle to an indirect tax on cigarettes.

A recent criminal case involving a Jenkins Act violation demonstrates how heavily the ability of a state to provide revenue by means of indirect taxation rests on the destination principle.[10] New York State imposes a tax on the sale or use of cigarettes[11] (at the time of the case, the rate was six cents for each ten cigarettes), and New York City levies its own additional cigarette tax in addition to the state rate. In May 1971, it was discovered that some 300,000 New Yorkers had been buying their cigarettes from North Carolina mail-order houses for several years. The sellers had not observed the provisions of the Jenkins Act, and none of the buyers had been asked by New York officials to pay cigarette tax (nor had the sellers withheld any tax). The amount of unpaid New York cigarette tax was estimated to be in the millions of dollars.

Conclusion

The attempt of the states to achieve complete implementation of the destination principle for their sales taxes provides a vivid illustration of the theoretical considerations laid out earlier in the chapter. A state needs this principle for indirect taxation in order to use its tax power most effectively. This is the main reason why the United States adopted the destination principle for sales taxes with respect to its internal trade[12] (whereas it opposes the application of this principle to international trade, as shown early in this study). The support the states, in their attempts to close loopholes in the destination principle, received by the highest constitutional organs of the United States—Congress (Jenkins Act), and Supreme Court (acceptance of the use tax)—reflects the respect of these organs for the states' tax power.

Taxation of Intracommunity Trade in a Future United Western Europe

The first step toward unification of indirect taxation in the EEC has been described in Chapter 1: all member states were directed to replace their general indirect taxes by a VAT of a certain uniform type. It is difficult to predict the exact nature of the next steps, especially considering that the first phase is not yet completed (Italy

still applies a turnover tax of the old type) and that the possible
enlargement of the EEC to a ten-member organization, comprising
most of Western Europe, may pose many unexpected problems. But
the Commission of the EEC has already made tentative plans for the
future, and they are characterized by the following features:[13]

1. The tax rates of the member countries will be approximately
the same. (It may be noted that such uniformity would solve the problem of "direct imports" which has plagued the state tax authorities
in the United States.)

2. Exporters will no longer be exempt from the VAT. That
means that there will be no tax rebates on exported goods. The importer of a product (whether final or intermediate) will be allowed to
deduct from his tax liability the VAT paid for this product in the origin
country. In other words, there will be no special import tax. The
tax liabilities of individual producers or distributors are independent
of the origin or the destination of the product involved. (All this applies
only to intracommunity trade. External trade will continue to be
subject to the destination principle.)

3. The VAT levied on a certain product will accrue to the treasury
of the country where this product is consumed. A clearing system
will be devised in order to achieve this result. The national tax
administrations will compute the amount of tax paid to them for goods
that were exported and transfer the net balance to the destination
country.[14]

Point 3 demonstrates that the destination principle will, with
respect to VAT revenue, continue to be applied to intracommunity
trade. Thus, the power of the member states to tax consumption,
although heavily restricted by community agreements, will be respected
at least in its core.

Model Solutions for World Trade

It is remarkable that even federations that knit their member
states as close together as the United States today, and possibly United
Europe in the future, adhere to the destination principle for trade
between their member states, despite the fact that this principle entails
considerable administrative burdens. The reason has been indicated
above: indirect taxation can only be fully effective if the destination
principle is adopted. Thus, the United States and the EEC of the future
do in fact provide model solutions for world trade: international regulation should, if at all possible, follow the example of these federations and not restrict the right of trading nations to adhere to the
destination principle for their indirect taxes.

FINAL CONCLUSIONS

Origin Principle Versus Destination Principle: Policy Conclusions

General Taxes

The analysis of this chapter has produced two general conclusions. With respect to direct taxation, national tax power would be restricted less by the origin principle than by the destination principle; this result corresponds happily to the conclusion of Chapter 3 where it was said that the origin principle for this kind of taxation would better serve the economic interests of the world community. For indirect taxation, a country's tax sovereignty would be severely limited by the origin principle and much less so by the destination principle; again, this result happens to be in agreement with the conclusions of Chapter 3, where the destination principle was held to be preferable to the origin principle.

It might be argued that international regulation need only prescribe that each state has to make a binding decision between the origin and destination principle but need not mandate which principle is to be adopted. However, this course of action would be undesirable for several reasons:

1. The main reason is that balance of payments disruptions resulting from domestic tax changes are less likely if the origin principle for direct taxes and the destination principle for indirect taxes is implemented by all trading countries (see Chapter 3).

2. If all countries apply the destination principle to indirect taxes, the difference between the two currency exchange rates in effect created by this principle is generally smaller than if some countries adopt the origin principle. Consequently, the inducement of possibly undesirable factor movements is less significant.

3. It might be very difficult to prevent countries faced with a balance of payments deficit from switching from the origin principle to the destination principle, if their trading partners adhere to this latter principle. If all countries apply the same principle, the temptation to cure balance of payments difficulties by a switch to the other principle will be smaller. It is always easier for a country to defend its action if it does the same as other nations already do than if it takes an unprecedented action.

Selective Taxes

Even more than in the case of general taxation, national tax sovereignty would be severely limited, in some cases all but paralyzed, if a country were forced to adopt the origin principle for indirect taxes and the destination principle for direct taxation. This realization has to be weighed against the finding of Chapter 3 that the economic interest of the trading community would best be served by 50 percent adjustments. The reasoning of this chapter's discussion of the destination versus origin principle and especially the observations made with respect to federations suggest that the national interest has to be given more weight than the efficiency considerations. This is particularly so because the border adjustment rate that would be ideal from the efficiency point of view cannot be determined exactly, and 50 percent would represent a rather crude solution—possibly quite removed from the most efficient situation. Therefore, the principles applied to selective taxation should be the same as those implemented for general taxation: the origin principle for direct taxes and the destination principle for indirect taxes.

To leave the choice between the two principles to the individual countries would (as in the case of general taxes) not be advisable, for the following two reasons:

1. If all countries adopted the destination principle for indirect taxes, maximization of production would be achieved internationally, at the cost of distorting optimum trade. If two trading countries were to implement opposite principles for the same good, neither optimization of trade nor maximization of production would occur. The inefficiencies created by one of the two principles would add to those resulting from the other.

2. Sudden switches from one principle to the other would be less likely to occur if all countries without exception bound themselves to adhere to the same principle.

Border Tax Adjustments and Other Levy/Subsidy Systems Distinguished

Now, at the end of the search for "ideal" border tax adjustments, some observations regarding the nature of these adjustments can be made. The preceding sections of this chapter showed that the origin principle for direct taxes and the destination principle for indirect taxes are generally indispensably connected with national tax sovereignty. Therefore, the "ideal" system of import taxes and export rebates should be regarded as part of the domestic tax system, and not as an independent instrument of foreign economic policy.

Introduction of a levy/subsidy system the rates of which do not correspond to the country's domestic indirect tax should not be referred to as a change in border tax adjustments but as a parity change restricted to the trade account. If a country labels this limited parity change as "border tax adjustments," it simply tries to disguise the real nature of the scheme in order not to be exposed to domestic criticism of the kind that may accompany an alteration of the currency exchange rate. This is what West Germany did in 1968 when it introduced 4 percent levies on most exports and 4 percent subsidies on most imports in the form of a change in the border adjustments for the turnover tax.[15] Inasmuch as the domestic tax rate (11 percent VAT) was not altered, the effect was an upward revaluation of the West German currency by 4 percent, limited to trade in goods. A mislabeling of this kind must be rejected as a political gimmick. Moreover, it tends to have undesirable side-effects, which the legislature may not even be aware of. For example, the West German "border tax adjustment change" of 1968 mirrored the structure of the domestic VAT and made a difference between the goods subject to an 11 percent domestic tax and those on which only 5.5 percent was levied. For the former, the new levy/subsidy rate was 4 percent (which meant a reduction of the previous adjustments to 7 percent); for the latter, it was only 2 percent (reduction to 3.5 percent). This seemed only natural in that "border adjustments" generally reflect the domestic tax rate. But it was a senseless measure in the new context, because government and legislature wanted to achieve a disguised revaluation. The consequence of the new law was that imports of the vast majority of goods were encouraged by 4 percent subsidies. This tended to keep domestic prices down and control inflation. Imports of the privileged necessities, however, were less encouraged (only by 2 percent subsidies), so that the price effect benefiting domestic consumers was bound to be smaller in this case. As a result, the socially motivated difference between necessities of life and other goods, which the domestic tax law made, was weakened by the new law. This undesirable effect would have been avoided by a uniform 4 percent levy/subsidy system for all traded goods, or by an outright 4 percent revaluation.

Although a levy/subsidy system designed to safeguard the balance of payments must strictly be distinguished from border tax adjustments and has to be regarded as a de facto parity change (limited to trade), its legal nature is much closer to that of a tax adjustment than to that of a currency exchange rate alteration. Like tax laws, a levy/subsidy system necessitates, in almost all Western democracies, an act of the legislature, whereas parity changes are in most countries effected

solely by the executive power.* A levy/subsidy system is usually
introduced by an ordinary statute, similar to a tax law, whereas the
legal nature of a parity change almost eludes precise definition: the
change is effected by an order directed at the country's central bank
to step into the foreign exchange market at a certain point.

---

*The United States is a notable exception. Switzerland recently
altered its pertinent law and empowered government to change the
parity without legislative action. It was felt that this was necessary
in order to keep the usual speculation preceding a parity change down
to a minimum. The Swiss Government used its new power very soon
and appreciated the Swiss Franc in May 1971. In Great Britain, parity
changes are considered a privilege of the Crown. In West Germany,
all currency exchange rate changes to date have been effected by the
government, not by parliament, although the law is not clear at this
point.

PART

III

**THE PRESENT
INTERNATIONAL LAW
OF BORDER TAX ADJUSTMENTS**

6

THE RULES
ON BORDER TAX ADJUSTMENTS
IN THE GENERAL AGREEMENT
ON TARIFFS AND TRADE:
INTERPRETATION AND CRITICISM

INTRODUCTION

The Pattern of Border Tax Adjustment
Rules in GATT

The GATT rules dealing with border tax adjustments are scattered through the General Agreement. The border tax regulation has been divided into various single provisions which then are distributed to at least seven different Articles. These Articles deal, in each case, with many other questions as well, and one cannot comprehend the border tax law of GATT through a cursory reading of its provisions. Without yet judging the soundness of the GATT rules, it is obvious that a separate Article dealing with all aspects of border tax adjustments would be preferable to the present pattern.

In Appendix II of this book, an attempt is made to bring the scattered GATT provisions into order. The rules dealing with taxation of imports are comprised in one group, those applicable to taxation of exports in another.

The Geographical Expansion of
the GATT Tax Law

The major trading nations in the nonsocialist world—the countries of Western Europe and North America, and Japan—are members ("Contracting Parties") of the General Agreement on Tariffs and Trade. About fifty other countries, including a few states belonging to the socialist orbit, are also members.[1]

However, not all of these nations have fully adopted the GATT's provisions on border tax adjustments. As already mentioned, there

are several single rules scattered through the General Agreement.
One of them—the prohibition of export subsidies for nonprimary goods
in Article XVI (4)—has been adopted only by certain industrial
countries, whereas almost all less-developed nations have refused to
sign it.2 Thus, the GATT law of border tax adjustments is fully in
force for the United States, Canada, Japan, and most Western European
countries, including the EEC members and Great Britain. The other
Contracting Parties are subject to all border tax adjustment rules
except Article XVI (4).

INTERPRETING THE GATT RULES ON
BORDER TAX ADJUSTMENTS

"Legal technicalities rather than economic realities have
long been dominant. . . . The economist often feels that
lawyers and the courts have concentrated on the letter of
the law, without defining its spirit with any precision."

The above statements, which Paul A. Samuelson made with
respect to U.S. antitrust law,3 hint at the basic problems encountered
in any interpretation of legal rules designed to regulate economic
activity. Perhaps in this more than any other field of law, the lawyer
may be led astray by his tendency to attribute independent values to
certain words or expressions of a statute instead of focusing on the
underlying policy. Moreover, precise determination of the policy
that is to guide the lawyer may be an even more formidable problem
than adherence to it.
       In the case of GATT's tax law, the basic question in the search
for policies guiding the interpretation is the following: To what
extent should the intent of the Contracting Parties be taken into
account—the historical intent, as revealed in the voluminous preparatory work to GATT, and the present intent, as reflected in the current
border tax practice? This question touches one of the fundamental
problems of all interpretation. It is far from settlement in national
legal systems, let alone in international law. Answering it requires
a value judgment. The lawyer who favors stability and certainty will
tend to adhere to the historical intent of the creator of the legal rules
(although it is questionable whether stability and certainty are in
fact served by such an adherence). However, if law is regarded as
a force designed to shape an economic system and society, it seems
inconceivable that the meaning of a statute should remain inflexible
in view of constant economic and social change. This leads to the
understanding of a statute or international regulation as a legal
phenomenon gaining its own independent life, once created, and perhaps

assuming different meanings in the context of different stages of
economic or social development.

Adherence to this "flexible" method of interpretation, in contrast to the "historical" construction which seeks to ascertain the
intent of the lawmaker, is even more justified in the case of GATT
than in that of any other international agreement. First, only a small
part of the present GATT members participated in the preparatory
work. Most Contracting Parties adhered to GATT in the 1950s or
1960s, and little if anything is known about their interpretation of the
border tax adjustment rules at the time of their adherence. Second,
current practices do not necessarily reflect a country's interpretation
of the GATT rules. For example, West Germany for a long time
applied "undercompensating" border adjustments, gradually adopting
full adjustments only in recent years. Clearly, this did not prove
that Germany came to attribute a different meaning to the GATT rules
on border tax adjustments. Rather, the reason was that domestic
business had lobbied for the change (see Chapter 1). Another example
is the the U.S. application of the destination principle to international
trade with respect to its indirect taxes (federal excises as well as
state sales taxes) and the origin principle with respect to its direct
taxes. However, it officially doubts whether this reflects a correct
interpretation of GATT (see Chapter 2).

Whereas international law is devoid of generally acknowledged
rules of interpretation, some tendencies can be discerned in theory
as well as in practice. There are many indications today that multilateral agreements are interpreted in a less "historical" way than
bilateral treaties, especially when they have created international
organizations.[4] The main reason is that the more parties there are
to consider, the more difficult it is to ascertain what the parties
themselves really meant by a certain clause in an agreement.

Interpreting GATT's rules on border tax adjustments in a
"flexible" way does not, of course, mean that the interpreter may
substitute his own, arbitrary policy goals for those of the General
Agreement. The preamble to GATT is quite explicit in stating the
relevant policies that underly all the Articles: "raising standards of
living, ensuring full employment and a large and steadily growing
volume of real income and effective demand, developing the full use
of the resources of the world and expanding the production and exchange of goods."

These are obviously exactly the same policies that have been
considered in Part II of this study. "Developing the full use of resources of the world and expanding the production and exchange of
goods" restates the goals of maximization of production and optimization
of trade (in this order), which were examined in Chapter 3. The other
policies enumerate the goals shown earlier to require that international

regulation of border tax adjustments (1) should secure equilibrium in all balances of international payments (Chapter 3) and (2) should not interfere with national economic and social policy more than is necessary in the interest of other countries (Chapter 5). A different meaning could be given to this sentence of GATT's preamble only if the interests of particular countries at the cost of other nations were to be pursued rather than the interests of the trading community as a whole. This, however, is ruled out by the second sentence of the preamble: "Being desirous of contributing to these objectives by entering into reciprocal and mutually advantageous arrangements directed to . . . the elimination of discriminatory treatment in international commerce."

In addition to the preamble, there exists one other guideline for interpretation of GATT's tax law. The traditional principle that international agreements should be interpreted in the way that does the least harm to national sovereignty—challenged as often as defended[5]—is a sensible principle at least with regard to border tax adjustments. The reason has been demonstrated in Chapter 5. International economic regulation designed to enhance economic welfare defeats its own purpose if it so interferes with national tax power that welfare in all countries consequently decreases.

Thus, the policies to be taken into account in any interpretation of the GATT rules on border tax adjustments happen to be exactly the same policies pursued in Part II's search for "ideal" taxation of internationally traded goods. This means that, as long as the words permit it, GATT should be interpreted in a way yielding the same results achieved in Part II.

BORDER ADJUSTMENTS FOR GENERAL TAXES

Border Adjustments for General Indirect Taxes

Exports

Article VI (4) and Ad Article XVI, in almost identical words, permit exemption of an exported good from taxes "borne by the like product when destined for domestic consumption" (or refund of such taxes).

In Part II it has been demonstrated that all countries should adopt the destination principle for general indirect taxes* This

---

*See "Border Tax Adjustments and Economic Efficiency" in Chapter 3. Inasmuch as not only indirect taxes levied on the final stage of

referred to the "pure" application of the destination principle, which means exemption of exports from all indirect taxes whatsoever, including taxes on inputs used in the manufacturing process (the term "input" being used in a wide sense, comprising not only raw material or semimanufactured products, but also investment goods such as plant or machinery, and auxiliary materials such as vehicles and fuel for transportation).*

Consequently, the term "borne by a domestic product" must be interpreted to include all stages of production prior to exportation. All taxes on inputs (in this wide sense) are "borne" by the final good. Estimations are necessary if the amount of this total indirect tax burden cannot exactly be determined, as in the case of a cumulative turnover tax. These estimations are bound to breed controversy, and the current universal trend toward the adoption of the VAT and single-stage taxes is about to remove one of the inevitable problems of international regulation of border tax adjustments.

Chapters 3 and 4 showed that the phrase "borne by" should in no event be understood to mean that tax rebates on exports are to reflect the actual degree of tax shifting, although this interpretation would perhaps be buttressed more than any other by the "ordinary meaning" of the words. What is decisive is not the ordinary meaning but the meaning the words assume when they are read with certain specific policies in mind.

With respect to exports of intermediate goods—i.e., goods that are not immediately sold for consumption but are used by producers of finished products in the destination country—Part II established that they should be treated in exactly the same way as final goods, which means that they should also be relieved of all indirect tax whatsoever. This is mandated by economic theory (see Chapter 3 on "Exportation of Intermediate Goods") as well as by practical considerations, in that it will sometimes be difficult to determine whether an exported good is immediately consumed in the destination country or whether it is used there as an input.

---

production but also those imposed on inputs (in a wide sense) tend to have a price-raising effect, the term "destination principle" referred to the "pure" application of this principle also in the context of the balance of payments considerations and the problem of national fiscal sovereignty.

*See Chapter 3, "Preliminary Conclusions," and Chapter 5, "Final Conclusions."

If the term "borne by" is interpreted in the way described and if the word "product" is understood to refer to intermediate as well as to final good, GATT permits—with respect to general indirect taxation—application of the destination principle to exports in accordance with the conclusions of Part II.

Imports

Article III (2) permits countries to subject imported goods to internal taxes that are "applied, directly or indirectly, to like domestic products."

In Part II it was demonstrated that the indirect tax levied on imported goods should exactly equal the total indirect tax imposed on the same good when it is produced domestically. "Total" tax means the full amount of the "wedge" put between the final price and the income of the productive factors, i.e., it includes the indirect tax on inputs used in the manufacturing process—even that on durable investment goods and auxiliary materials.* Thus, the correct interpretation of "applied to" is in effect the same as that of "borne by." Indirect taxes on inputs (in the wide sense) are not applied directly to the final product, to be sure. But Article III (2) explicitly refers as well to those taxes "indirectly" applied to the final good. And Article II (2) (a) clearly permits levying on imported goods taxes that are imposed domestically on inputs from which these goods are made.

In the case of a VAT or single-stage turnover tax, the exact tax burden to be put on imports is indicated by the tax rate. If a country applied a cumulative turnover tax, the familiar problem of estimation arises. Estimates are also necessary when a selective indirect tax is levied on a certain input only (e.g., gasoline). If thereby all final products are affected to about the same extent, this selective tax must be treated like a general tax on finished goods, and the estimated rate must be applied to imports.

Imported intermediate goods must be taxed in exactly the same way as domestic inputs (see Chapter 3, "Importation of Intermediate Goods"). That is, all indirect taxes applied domestically at stages of production through which the imported good has already passed in the origin country must be added and levied at the border on inputs. If domestic inputs are not taxed at all, as under a retail sales tax, the

---

*If the "pure" destination principle is pursued for exports, it must also be applied to imports, in that the optimization of trade requires that the rate of border tax adjustments is the same for exports and imports (see Chapter 3).

import tax is, of course, zero. At all stages subsequent to importation, products manufactured (partly) from imports must be taxed
exactly as wholly domestic goods are.

If the term "applied to" is interpreted in the way indicated and
if the word "product" is again understood to include intermediate
goods, GATT permits (with respect to general indirect taxes) application of the destination principle to imports in accordance with the
principles set out in Part II.

The Taxe Occulte Problem

Taxe occulte ("hidden tax") is a term that has assumed considerable prominence in the discussion of border tax adjustments. It
refers to the "hidden" elements of tax paid in respect of goods (or
services) used in the production or transportation of the finished product, especially to indirect tax on capital equipment goods (machinery,
vehicles) and auxiliary materials (fuel). These taxes are not easily
allocable to the final goods—a fact that has led many to conclude that
there should be no import levies or export rebates for taxe occulte.

The opponents of taxe occulte adjustments have received support
by the EEC Court of Justice. As already noted in Chapter 1, the rules
on border tax adjustments in the Rome Treaty correspond closely to
those of GATT. The EEC provisions use the term "directly or
indirectly" not only in the case of imports (as GATT does) but also
in the case of exports.[6] In Case 45/64 (EEC Commission v. Italy),
the EEC Court of Justice ruled that under Article 96 (taxation of
exports), "the expression 'directly' should be understood as relating
to taxes which are imposed on the finished good, while the term
'indirectly' relates to taxes imposed at different stages of production
on the raw materials or semi-finished products used in the manufacture
of the product."[7] The Court consequently held that taxes on motor
cars used by the producing firms were not to be rebated to exporters.

Several years after the decision in Case 45/64, the corresponding
question with respect to imports came before the Court. This time
the words of the judgment were less clear. Significantly, the Court
made no reference at all to its earlier judgment concerning exports.
From this, it has been concluded that the Court tried to limit the
impact of its decision in Case 45/64.[8] Indeed, the pending introduction
of the VAT in the entire EEC practically required a change in the
Court's attitude, in that the VAT rate contains taxe occulte and it
would mean renouncing the advantages of the VAT if new estimations—
subtracting the taxe occulte from the VAT—were to be introduced for
international trade. The present border adjustments in the EEC,
applying the full VAT rates, have not been challenged before the Court.

Even disregarding the apparent shift in the Court's attitude,
Case 45/64 should not be used as a precedent for the interpretation
of GATT. The above discussion of exports and imports has established—
on the basis of Part II—that adjustments should also be made for
taxe occulte.

Flexibility of the Adjustment Rate

The result of the examination of GATT thus far is the following:
GATT can, and should, be interpreted as permitting application of the
destination principle to general indirect taxes. The VAT of the EEC
countries and the state sales taxes in the United States follow this
principle and are, therefore, sanctioned by GATT.

However, the conclusion reached in Part II with respect to
general indirect taxes was that international regulation should
prescribe adoption of the destination principle by all countries (see
Chapter 5). Comparison of this result with the pertinent GATT rules—
Article III (2) for imports and Article VI (4) for exports—immediately
reveals one of the major deficiencies of GATT's tax law. GATT
merely subjects border tax adjustments to a limitation (they may not
exceed the tax applied to domestic products) and consequently permits
any rate of adjustment between zero and this limit. Thus, a country
is at liberty to adopt the origin principle for indirect taxes. Also,
there appears to be no way to read into GATT a prohibition of frequent
changes in border tax adjustment rates within the prescribed limits.
This means that GATT allows countries (within certain limits) to
operate levy/subsidy systems unconnected with domestic tax changes.
There is no international control over the application of these schemes
that would be comparable to the supervision of parity changes by the
IMF. This is, without doubt, an undesirable feature of the current
law. It not only endangers the stability which the present system of
fixed exchange rates and IMF control over parity changes is designed
to achieve, but it also favors countries with high indirect tax rates
over other nations.

Border Adjustments for General
Direct Taxes

Part II concluded that the origin principle should be applied to
general direct taxes (especially income taxes). This result is
compatible with GATT.

Imports

The term "applied to products" in Article III (2) has to be interpreted in a formal way. It refers only to taxes computed with respect to goods, i.e., "indirect taxes" as defined at the beginning of Chapter 1. This means that, under GATT, a country is not allowed to levy direct taxes on imported finished goods.

In the case of intermediate products, a country bound by GATT may—and should—apply its direct tax on all stages of production subsequent to the importation, but no special import tax should be levied on the input when it is imported.*

Exports

The term "borne by products" in Article VI (4) and Ad Article XVI must also be interpreted as referring to indirect taxes only. Given this interpretation, GATT in principle mandates adoption of the origin principle for general indirect taxes.

However, one peculiar feature of the GATT regulation must be noted. Exemption of exports from direct taxes is prohibited by Article XVI (4) only if this "results in the sale of such product for export at a price lower than the comparable price charged for the like product to buyers in the domestic market." Income tax exemption (or rebates) for all export business need not necessarily entail such a price difference. Moreover, as stated earlier, Article XVI (4) has been adopted only by relatively few countries. In all other cases—that is, when export prices are not lowered, or when the country is not bound by Article XVI (4)—Article VI applies. This Article contains no outright prohibition of direct tax exemptions of exports (or corresponding rebates). But it provides countries that are economically injured (Article VI), 6a) by such exemptions or rebates with a powerful defensive weapon: they may levy countervailing duties (Article VI, 3).

Current Practices

At present, many countries apply income tax schemes that enable export business to escape the full weight of the domestic income tax in one way or another.[9] These countries, in effect, partially implement the destination principle for general direct taxes. Inasmuch as they do not levy special direct taxes on imports nor completely

---

*This is a consequence of the origin principle. See Chapter 3, "Border Tax Adjustments and Economic Efficiency."

free all exports from direct taxes, the origin principle remains intact to a large extent. Special income tax treatment of the export business is of two kinds:

1. Some countries do not tax a manufacturer's income from exports at all, or apply a lower rate. A well-known example is Ireland which for many years has conducted a heavy advertisement campaign in foreign newspapers, attracting the attention of foreign investors to the fact that it does not tax income from exports for 15 years after a new firm has begun production. Ireland is a member of GATT but has not adopted Article XVI (4). Consequently, this tax scheme cannot be challenged as violative of GATT. However, countries that are injured may apply countervailing duties.

2. Another scheme is more widely used. Many of the large trading nations grant income tax privileges to subsidiaries through which manufacturing companies conduct their export sales. An example of such a tax scheme is provided by the proposal of a "Domestic International Sales Corporation" in the United States.[10] This proposal has been suggested by the Administration and is presently being considered by Congress. It provides for an amendment of the Internal Revenue Code that would create a new category of domestic corporation to be known as a Domestic International Sales Corporation (DISC). The U.S. tax on the export income derived through such a corporation would be deferred as long as it is either used in the corporation's export business or invested in "export-related assets" of the DISC, and thus not distributed to the DISC shareholders. "Export-related assets" would include loans to manufacturers (including the DICS's U.S. parent company of which the DISC is a subsidiary) to finance investments in U.S. plant, equipment and machinery, inventory, and research and development to the extent that these investments are deemed export related. In order to qualify as a DISC, a corporation would be required to confine its activities almost entirely to export selling.

Article XVI (4), which has been adopted by the United States, would prohibit the DISC income tax scheme only if its effect were a reduction in export prices in relation to domestic prices. A price effect of this kind could well occur: It has been estimated that the U.S. Treasury would lose $500 million annually in income tax receipts because of the DISC arrangement.[11] It is difficult to believe that none of the $500 million in reduced Treasury receipts would be used, at least in part, to improve the sales prices of American products. If there were no such price effect, the United States would be free to go ahead with DISC, but foreign countries would be allowed, under certain circumstances, to retaliate with countervailing duties (Article VI).

BORDER ADJUSTMENTS FOR
SELECTIVE TAXES

Border Adjustments for Selective
Indirect Taxes

Part II has demonstrated that the destination principle should be adopted for selective indirect taxes. Inasmuch as GATT does not distinguish between general and selective taxes, it permits application of the destination principle to both of them.* Whereas the technical questions are generally the same in the case of general and selective indirect taxes, the latter give rise to two peculiar problems.

Multiple Exchange Rates

Chapter 4 demonstrated that application of general border tax adjustments—e.g., those practiced by the VAT countries—can be regarded as institution of multiple exchange rates. The official parity applies to capital transactions, whereas the exchange rate as modified by the border tax adjustment applies to trade. In developing this thought even further, it could be argued that there are more than just these two exchange rates. If a country subjects a group of commodities to a special indirect tax in addition to its general tax—as most VAT countries do—the economic effect could be regarded as a third exchange rate, applying to trade in these selected goods.

The Agreement of the International Monetary Fund (Article VIII, 3), to which most GATT members are parties, prohibits "multiple currency practices." Superficially, it may seem that application of the destination principle to selective indirect taxes is in conflict with this rule. But it must be recalled that, in Chapter 4, the equation of border tax adjustments to a modification of the official parity was used in order to show the fallacy of international cost comparisons. For this purpose only, the link between these adjustments and the domestic tax was neglected. Chapter 5, however, demonstrated the crucial importance of this link. Border tax adjustments must be seen as a part of the national tax system, not as an independent levy/subsidy system at the border. Therefore, they cannot—except for certain didactic purposes—be equated to (limited) parity changes.

---

*Again, the fact that GATT does not mandate the destination principle is one of the major deficiencies of its tax law.

Consequently, they cannot be regarded as "multiple currency practices" within the scope of the IMF prohibition.

Tariffs in the Guise of Selective Indirect Taxes

If a selective indirect tax is levied on a good not produced at all in the taxing country (e.g., coffee, bananas), the economic effect is exactly the same as if a tariff were imposed on that good. A tax of this kind should, therefore, be treated in international regulation (and in negotiations) as a customs duty.

The same is true if the good subject to the selective tax is economically a substitute for a good that is not taxed. For example, a country may tax petroleum but not coal. Thereby, it in effect protects its coal industry from the competition of the (domestic and foreign) petroleum industry. The considerations of Part II do not fit this particular problem. Rather, the situation is very close to that created by a tariff: foreign exporters are faced with a barrier designed to protect the domestic industry. The only difference is that a tariff on a certain good ordinarily protects the domestic industry producing this very good, whereas in the situation just described a different industry is protected. Thus, taxes of this kind should be dealt with like tariffs. International negotiations should attempt to achieve first their "binding" and then their gradual removal.

GATT generally prohibits selective taxes that protect domestic production (Article III, 2, and Ad Article III). This prohibition does not seem to have been effective, and many violations have been reported.[12] For the reasons given above, a regulation equating such taxes to tariffs would be preferable.

Border Adjustments for Selective Direct Taxes

In the closing section of Chapter 3, policy suggestions were offered for the case where a country favors a certain industry (e.g., the shipbuilding industry) by income tax reductions. The following two alternative suggestions were made: (1) the country should tax exports and subsidize imports of the respective good; and (2) other trading nations should tax imports of the respective good from that country and subsidize exports of this good to it.

In most cases, a country that has adopted a selective direct tax will not tax exports or subsidize imports, although it would be free to do so under GATT.* The country is not required to take this course of action; GATT does not prohibit domestic subsidies (there is only a requirement in Article XVI, 1, to notify the Contracting Parties of the subsidy). Thus, as a practical matter, only the second suggestion is a realistic possibility.

GATT does not allow countries to apply countervailing export subsidies in such a case (Article XVI, 4). This is a deficiency of the present regulation. It does, however, permit countervailing duties (Article VI). The requirement of injury in Article VI (6) (a) of GATT corresponds to the policy conclusion reached at the very end of Chapter 3.

VIOLATIONS AND REMEDIES

International regulation of border tax adjustments will only be effective when it can be enforced in one way or other. This section is not intended to offer a profound treatment of the problem hereby raised. Rather, its purpose is to demonstrate the range of possible remedies in the case of a violation of GATT's tax rules and to give some indications of the desirable improvement of the present enforcement procedures.

Remedies Available to States

GATT Procedures

The GATT provisions on consultation, complaints, and enforcement[13] offer the principal way of settling international disputes about border tax adjustments. Their major deficiency is the absence of a burden-of-proof provision. Especially in the case of selective taxes, it is very difficult for other countries to ascertain the actual impact of the tax on certain internationally traded goods. The taxing country should be obliged to furnish information if the question of a GATT

---

*GATT allows export taxes and import subsidies not only in the case of a selective direct tax but quite generally. This could lead to economically undesirable results if countries would ever take such action. Apparently the framers of GATT never thought of this possibility. They probably adhered to the traditional mercantilistic view— "imports are bad for a country, exports good." As long as this view is taken, export taxes and import subsidies will seldom occur.

violation is raised. This would put only a small administrative burden
on the alleged culprit but would considerably assist countries
contemplating the initiation of GATT complaint procedures.

World Court Jurisdiction

A well-known case of an alleged violation of GATT border tax
adjustment rules is the "Whisky Case." U.S. importers of Irish and
Scotch whisky claim that the United States in effect levies a higher
excise tax on imported distilled spirits than on domestic ones. The
problem has often been dealt with in the United States, in legal proceedings as well as in scholarly writings.[14] The Courts have per-
sistently held that GATT is not violated. After each unfavorable
court decision, the importers have waited a few years and then again
challenged the validity of the respective taxing practice. In the most
recent case, the British Government—concerned about exports of
Scotch whisky—supported the appeal to the U.S. Supreme Court as
amicus curiae.[15] After the Supreme Court had denied certiorari,[16]
the attorney for the importers filed a petition for rehearing, asking
the Supreme Court to rule on the dispute so that the World Court would
have a decision of the highest court in the United States to review.[17]
The Supreme Court apparently was not impressed by the implicit
threat to bring the United States before the World Court, accusing it
of persistent violation of GATT, and denied the petition.[18]

Informing the Supreme Court that the case it refused to hear
might be taken to the World Court at the Hague may have been just a
tactical maneuver of the attorney for plaintiffs. It is not certain
whether the World Court could actually consider the case. First,
only states may be parties in cases before the court.[19] Second, even
if Great Britain should decide to take this step, the question arises
whether the World Court has jurisdiction over the United States in a
case of this kind.

Remedies Available to Businessmen

Challenge of Domestic Tax Assessments

In many countries, importers and exporters may challenge the
legality of taxes imposed on them. If the tax assessment is in
accordance with domestic law but violative of GATT, the problem of
GATT's interaction with national legal systems arises. Often, a
domestic statute violating GATT will be regarded as valid by domestic
courts, whether it has been enacted before or after the country's
adoption of GATT.[20] But in some cases states have chosen to accord

higher status to GATT than to domestic statutes. For example, the U.S. Internal Revenue Code of 1954 provides that its rules shall not apply if they are contrary to an international treaty obligation of the United States.[21] Another example is Article 25 of West Germany's Basic Law, which provides that the "general rules of international law" supersede domestic statutes. It could be argued that some of GATT's border tax adjustment rules have become "general rules of international law."[22] If the domestic law of a country contains a provision of this kind, businessmen will be able to challenge tax assessments as violative of GATT even though national law is not violated. This can be a very effective way of enforcing a country's obligations under GATT.

Expropriation Damages

In some countries, businessmen injured by a change in the government's foreign economic policy may claim damages from the state if they had valid reasons to rely upon further pursuance of the previous policy.[23] An obligation imposed on the country by GATT rules to adhere to a certain policy may furnish a valid justification for such reliance. For example, if international regulation would require that imports be subjected to the same tax as domestic goods (which it presently does not), a producer injured by a sudden decrease in the import tax rate on competing products may have the right to claim damages from the government—a kind of expropriation damages, in that he loses part of his business.

Countervailing Duties

Present countervailing duty statutes usually confer no right on businessmen to demand countervailing duties if a country is allowed to apply them under GATT.[24] To establish such a right would probably mean a serious interference with a country's freedom to pursue foreign economic policy, in that application of countervailing duties, even if justified by GATT, may provoke political reactions in other countries.

MAXIMIZATION OF PRODUCTION
VERSUS OPTIMIZATION OF TRADE:
A COMPROMISE SOLUTION
FOR SELECTIVE INDIRECT TAXES

The analysis in this Appendix is designed to explain the statements made in the "Compromise Solution" of Chapter 3.

THE MODELS USED FOR THE ANALYSIS

In the following analysis, it is possible to focus attention on the taxing country in that it is here that the welfare losses associated with the tax originate. If country A levies a selective tax of the origin type on the import-competing good a, production of a will cease to be maximized: A and B together could have more of a without having less of another product. The reason is that A produces not enough of a. A duty levied in A on the import of a would have the desired result: by raising the price of a in A, production in A could be induced to increase to its previous level. However, this duty interferes with the optimization of trade. Consumers in A face a different price ratio than that prevailing under free trade, and consequently they consume less of a than previously. If they would consume the same as before the imposition of the duty—which would be the case if demand for a were completely inelastic in A—the conditions for maximum efficiency of the world economy would not be interfered with. This brief analysis shows that the two alternative welfare losses occuring in A, the production loss and the consumption loss, can be used to measure the impact of the tax on the entire world economy. Focusing attention on the changes in A does not mean that a national viewpoint is now adopted. This would require a measurement of the welfare changes resulting from the influence of A's tax on its terms of trade with B. It has been pointed out in the Introduction to Part II that such a nationalistic approach cannot lead to valid conclusions for economic policy in that countervailing or retaliatory action of other countries would have to be taken into account. The following considerations are, therefore, again based on the assumption that maximum efficiency of the world economy, and not simply a national advantage, is the desired goal.

The reason why a compromise between the two conflicting policies—optimum trade and maximized production—might be preferable to consistent pursuit of either of them can be seen most easily by means of a geometric model similar to that commonly used to show the harm done by a tariff.[1] The production loss and consumption loss are not only immediately visible in these models but, more important, conclusions regarding the relative magnitude of either loss can be drawn from the figures.[2]

The analysis will first be given for the "small country" case, i.e., the taxing country A is assumed to be unable to influence its terms of trade. The world price of each good is an invariable fact. The qualifications necessary once this assumption is dropped will be elaborated thereafter. In each case, one country (the taxing country) and one particular good is considered.

THE "SMALL COUNTRY" CASE:
FIXED WORLD PRICES

Domestic Tax on an Import-Competing Good

In Figure 1, domestic supply and demand are drawn on the basis of arbitrary assumptions, as is the world price of the selected good under consideration. The imports of the country are measured by ED when no tax is imposed. If now a tax implementing the origin principle is imposed, the domestic supply curve shifts upward by the amount of the tax. The product can still freely be imported at the old price, and no domestic price rise results. Consequently, consumption remains unchanged while production is cut back from E to A. Imports increase by the same amount. Whereas the cost to the country of producing the amount AE of the good was previously indicated by the quadrangle AFGE (the area under the supply curve), it is now indicated by the square AHGE, because this is what the country pays for its additional imports (by exports of many kinds of goods). The difference between the two quadrangles, which is hatched vertically in Figure 1, measures the cost of the tax to the country— a "production cost," caused by the misallocation of productive factors that is associated with a violation of the condition for maximized production.

Now a first step toward the destination principle is taken: imports of the good are taxed, not as heavily as domestically produced goods, but only at a smaller rate. The new situation is shown in Figure 1. The prime result is, of course, that the domestic price increases by the rate of the import tax. Production rises from A to

FIGURE 1

Domestic Tax on an Import-Competing Good

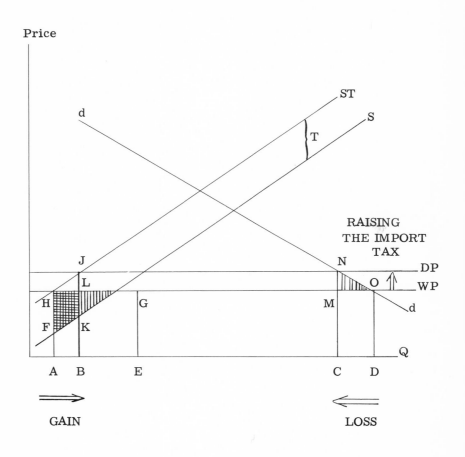

WP = world price

DP = domestic price = world price plus import tax

 S = supply before domestic tax

ST = supply after domestic tax

 T = domestic tax

 Q = quantity

B. The cost of AB, which was previously measured by AHLB because it was imported (and paid for by exports), decreases to AFKB (the area under the supply curve minus the tax, which is no cost to the country, in that it accrues to the domestic government). This means that a part of the production loss disappears (this part is hatched horizontally in Figure 1). In other words, the production loss diminishes. But simultaneously a change on the consumption side occurs: as the price of the good rises as a result of the small import tax, consumption decreases from D to C. The consumer surplus[3] shrinks by the triangle MNO, which stands for the resulting consumption loss (vertically hatched in Figure 1).

The peculiar connection between production loss and consumption loss in the case of a gradually increased import tax is now obvious: with the first introduction of a very small import tax, a large part of the production cost of the tax disappears, and a very small consumption loss develops simultaneously. With each successive rise of the import tax, the additional gain on the production side (which consists in the cancellation of the previous loss) becomes smaller and the additional loss on the consumption side larger.

A very small import tax is, therefore, clearly beneficial; the gain is big and the loss small. But in the process of gradually increasing the import tax, the point will be reached where the marginal gain on the production side just outweighs the marginal loss on the consumption side. Here the country should stop. But when will this point be reached? The import tax must be somewhere between zero and the domestic tax—this is the only definite answer, in that everything else depends upon the elasticities of supply and demand.

If the raising of the import tax is continued to the point where it equals the domestic tax, the entire production loss of the domestic tax is cancelled out, and only a consumption loss remains. This is the case of the pure destination principle, which does not misallocate resources but burdens the consumer by interfering with optimum trade. Figure 1 shows that it is impossible to compare the magnitudes of the welfare losses associated with either principle unless certain assumptions regarding the elasticities of supply and demand are made.[4] If domestic demand is totally inelastic, no consumption loss can result, and the destination principle is preferable. If, on the other hand, domestic supply happens to be completely inelastic, the origin principle is superior. Between these two limiting cases, the "ideal" import tax will be lower than the domestic tax but higher than zero. It will be the higher the less elastic domestic demand is, and the lower the less elastic domestic supply is.

Apart from the welfare changes that appear in Figure 1, a "medium" import tax which distributes the welfare loss resulting from the tax to production and consumption will have another advantage. Instead of one big distortion (production or consumption), there

will be two smaller distortions. The inertia of productive factors
and of consumers is often great enough that there is no response to
small changes in the circumstances. The tax might thus entail little
actual alteration in production or consumption, simply because old
habits are stronger than the small inducements produced by the tax.
If the entire impact of the tax falls on production or consumption,
this triumph of inertia is less likely, and distorting changes will actually take place.

Domestic Tax on an Exported Good

A corresponding analysis can be made for exported products
(Figure 2). This time, a domestic tax implementing the destination
principle shall be the starting point, in that this does not interfere at
all with free trade, as with the origin principle in the previous case
dealing with an import competing good. The destination principle
introduces a price difference between the taxing country and the rest
of the world. The world price remains unchanged, but the domestic
price increases by the amount of the tax. Inasmuch as the supply
curve for domestically consumed production shifts upward simultaneously by the same amount, no effect on production results. However, a decrease in domestic consumption accompanies the internal
price rise, entailing a consumption loss (vertically hatched in Figure
2: the triangle IKL).

Now a first step toward the origin principle is taken: an export
tax, smaller than the domestic tax, is introduced. As a result, the
domestic industry cannot maintain its access to the world market
at its present price. Production declines until the net price is below
the world price by the rate of the export tax, i.e., it declines from
E to D. A production loss results: if the country had exported DE,
it would have earned DFGE at a cost of DHGE. The difference, i.e.,
the triangle that measures the production loss, is hatched vertically
in Figure 2. However, the previous consumption loss is simultaneously reduced in that consumption increases as the domestic price
goes down. This gain (hatched horizontally in Figure 2) will outweigh
the production loss if the export tax is very small. With each successive rise of the export tax, the additional gain on the consumption
side becomes smaller and the additional loss on the production side
larger. At one point, where the export tax is between zero and the
full amount of the domestic tax, a further increase in the export will
no longer be accompanied by a net gain. As in the case of the import-
competing good, the amount of the "best" export tax depends upon
the elasticities of domestic supply and demand. If demand is totally
inelastic, the destination principle (zero export tax) would be ideal,

FIGURE 2

Domestic Tax on an Export Good

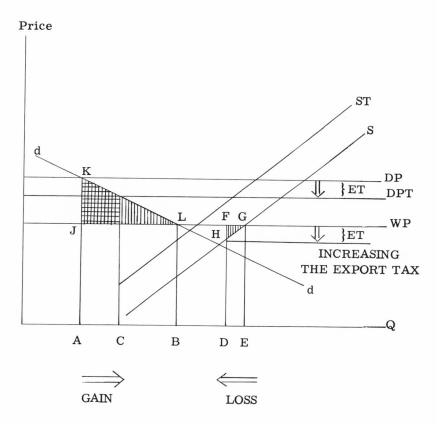

WP = world price

DP = domestic price

DPT = domestic price if export tax is applied

S = supply before domestic tax

ST = supply after domestic tax

ET = export tax

Q = quantity

in that no consumption loss results from the domestic tax. At the other end of the spectrum, the case of completely inelastic supply calls for the origin principle (full export tax). The less elastic domestic demand is, the lower should the export tax be. The less elastic domestic supply is, the more should the export tax approach the domestic tax rate. All this can easily be seen in Figure 2. The reader has only to change the demand and supply curves in his mind, i.e., imagine them to be steeper or flatter.

THE "BIG COUNTRY" CASE: ELASTICITIES OF FOREIGN SUPPLY AND DEMAND CONSIDERED

If foreign supply and demand are not assumed to be completely elastic, somewhat different conclusions must be drawn. For the great majority of countries and products, this qualification is without interest, but it cannot be doubted that some countries have monopsony or monopoly power at least in the trade of a few goods. For these exceptional circumstances, the following analysis is supplied.

Domestic Tax on an Import-Competing Good

The desired effect of an import tax, considered in the foregoing section, was achieved by means of the price rise connected with the introduction of this import tax. The more inelastic foreign supply is, the higher must the import tax be in order to achieve a certain desired domestic price rise. This can be seen in Figure 3. The "ideal" rate of import tax will, therefore, be the higher, the smaller the elasticity of supply from foreign countries is. It is possible, in an extreme case, that the "ideal" import tax is higher than the domestic tax. However, this is unlikely.[5]

Domestic Tax on an Exported Product

The desired effect of the export tax described above hinges on the reduction in the domestic price achieved by this tax. The more inelastic foreign demand for the good is, the more the world price rises when exports from the taxing country are curtailed, i.e., the higher must the export tax be in order to depress the domestic price sufficiently. A special case could call for taxation of exports higher than that of domestically consumed products but, again, such a case is not likely.[6]

FIGURE 3

The "Big Country" Case

Importing Country A   Export Supply and
                                      Import Demand

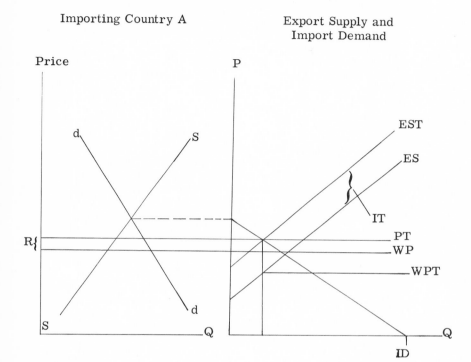

WP = world price before tax

WPT = world price after import tax

IT = A's import tax

P = price paid by the importer in A (in A's currency)

PT = A's price under import tax

ES = export supply

EST = export supply if A imposes import tax

Q = quantity

ID = import demand

R = desired price rise in A

RESULT

A selective indirect tax reduces the potential efficiency of the world economy by more if either the origin principle or destination principle is purely implemented than if a compromise between the two principles is adopted. It is preferable, therefore, to apply border tax adjustments at a rate between zero and the full domestic tax rate. A border rate that is half the domestic rate is likely to do less harm to world effeciency than a zero rate or a rate equal to the internal tax.

THE RULES ON TAXATION OF INTERNATIONALLY TRADED GOODS IN THE GENERAL AGREEMENT ON TARIFFS AND TRADE (GATT)

(These rules are scattered throughout the General Agreement. They are collected here and brought into some order. The letters used to establish this order, as well as the annotations in parentheses, do not belong to the General Agreement. The text reproduced here is the one that appears in the latest official version of GATT; see 4 BISD, 1969).

A (Tax Treatment of Imports)

a) <u>Article III: National Treatment on Internal Taxation</u>

1. The contracting parties recognize that internal taxes . . . should not be applied to imported . . . products so as to afford protection to domestic production.
2. The products of the territory of any contracting party imported into the territory of any other contracting party shall not be subject, directly or indirectly, to internal taxes . . . in excess of those applied, directly or indirectly, to like domestic products. Moreover, no contracting party shall otherwise apply internal taxes . . . to imported . . . products in a manner contrary to the principles set forth in paragraph 1.
. . .

b) <u>Article II: Schedule of Concessions</u>
. . .

2. Nothing in this Article shall prevent any contracting party from imposing at any time on the importation of any product:
(a) a charge equivalent to an internal tax imposed consistently with the provisions of a paragraph 2 of Article III in respect of the like domestic product or in respect of an

article from which the imported product has been manufactured or produced in whole or in part;
. . .

c) Article I: General Most-Favoured-Nation Treatment

1. . . . with respect to all matters referred to in paragraphs 2 . . . of Article III, any advantage . . . granted by
any contracting party to any product originating in or destined for any other country shall be accorded immediately
and unconditionally to the like product originating in or
destined for the territories of all other contracting parties.
. . .

d) Annex I: Notes and Supplementary Provisions
(The Annexes to the General Agreement contain authorita-
tive interpretations of some of the Articles.)

Ad Article III
Any internal tax . . . which applies to an imported product
and to the like domestic product and is collected or enforced in the case of the imported product at the time or
point of importation, is nevertheless to be regarded as an
internal tax . . . and is accordingly subject to the provisions of Article III.
. . .

Paragraph 2.
A tax conforming to the requirements of the first sentence
of paragraph 2 would be considered to be inconsistent with
the provisions of the second sentence only in cases where
competition was involved between, on the one hand, the
taxed product and, on the other hand, a directly competitive
or substitutable product which was not similarly taxed.
. . .

B (Tax Treatment of Exports)

a) Article XVI: Subsidies
aa) Section A - Subsidies in General

1. If any contracting party grants or maintains any subsidy, including any form of income or price support, which
operates directly or indirectly to increase exports of any
product from, or to reduce imports of any product into,
its territory, it shall notify the Contracting Parties . . .

bb) Section B - Additional Provisions on Export Subsidies

. . .

3. (This is a 1955 amendment which, since 1969, is in force for all Contracting Parties) . . . contracting parties should seek to avoid the use of subsidies on the export of primary products. . . .

4. (This provision applies only to a small number of Contracting Parties, including the United States, Canada, Japan, the EEC countries, and most of the EFTA countries, notably the United Kingdom. Almost none of the less-developed countries signed this provision.) . . . contrasting parties shall cease to grant either directly or indirectly any form of subsidy on the export of any product other than a primary product which subsidy results in the sale of such product for export at a price lower than the comparable price charged for the like product to buyers in the domestic market.

. . .

b) Annex I: Notes and Supplementary Provisions

Ad Article XVI

The exemption of an exported product from duties or taxes borne by the like product when destined for domestic consumption, or the remission of such duties or taxes in amounts not in excess of those which have accrued, shall not be deemed to be a subsidy.

. . .

c) Article VI: Anti-Dumping and Countervailing Duties
(The relationship of Articles XVI and VI is the following. The prohibition of subsidies is very limited. But even if GATT allows a subsidy, this does not mean that it prohibits other countries to defend themselves. They are allowed, under certain circumstances, to impose countervailing duties on subsidized imports.)

. . .

3. No countervailing duty shall be levied on any product of the territory of any contracting party imported into the territory of another contracting party in excess of an amount equal to the estimated bounty or subsidy determined to have been granted, directly or indirectly, on the manufacture, production or export of such product in the country of origin or exportation, including any special subsidy to the transportation of a particular product. The term "countervailing duty" shall be understood to mean a special duty levied for the purpose of offsetting any bounty or

subsidy bestowed, directly or indirectly, upon the manufacture, production or export of any merchandise.
4. No product of the territory of any contracting party
imported into the territory of any other contracting party
shall be subject to . . . countervailing duty by reason of
the exemption of such product from duties or taxes borne
by the like product when destined for consumption in the
country of origin or exportation, or by reason of the refund
of such duties or taxes.
. . .

6. (a) No contracting party shall levy any . . . countervailing duty on the importation of any product of the territory of another contracting party unless it determines
that the effect of the . . . subsidization . . . is such as to
cause or threaten material injury to an established domestic industry, or is such as to retard materially the establishment of a domestic industry.
. . .

CHAPTER 1

    1. The following figures show the share of indirect and direct taxes in the total tax revenue (all levels of government): Belgium— indirect 54 percent, direct 41 percent; France—indirect 58 percent, direct 39 percent; Italy—indirect 64 percent, direct 27 percent; West Germany—indirect 46 percent, direct 46 percent; United States—indirect 19 percent, direct 64 percent. In each case, the remainder is mainly provided by property taxes. (For indirect taxation in other European countries, see "The VAT in the New EEC Member States," and "The Spread of the VAT to Countries Outside the Common Market," later in this chapter.) United Nations Statistical Yearbook 1970 (U.S., figures for 1969), European Taxation, Vol. X, No. I (1970), p. 156 (EEC, 1967). International tax comparisons are necessarily inaccurate due to differences in classification and in compiling national data.

    2. See the statistics for 1967 in 16 AWD 199 (1970), Table III.

    3. Taxes as percentages of GNP (for the year 1970): France, 39 percent; West Germany, 35 percent; the United States, 29 percent. Paul A. Samuelson, Economics, New York: McGraw-Hill (8th ed., 1970), p. 141.

    4. The facts set out in this historical outline have mainly been drawn from: Günter Schmölders, "Steversystem und Steversystematik," Henry Laufenburger, "Die Einkommensbesteverung," Günter Schmölders, "Die Unsatzstevern" all in two Handbuch der Finanzwissenschaft, ed. Wilhelm Gerloff and Fritz Nevmark, second edition, Tübingen: Mohr, 1956; Günter Schmölders, Finanzpolitik, second edition, Berlin-Heidelberg-New York: Springer, 1965; Günter Schmölders, Allgemeine Steverlehre (fourth edition, Berlin: Duncker and Humblot, 1965); Gerd-Horst Pfeil, Steverreform als internationales problem (Berlin: Duncker and Humblot, 1955).

    5. A turnover tax can assume many different forms, but three types are most common:

    a. The turnover tax in the strict sense: collected at each point in the chain of distribution from manufacturer to retailer. The more stages, the more tax: the effect is a cumulative one. It is in this sense that the word is used in this study.

    b. The value-added tax (VAT). Each businessman pays as tax a certain percentage of the receipts from his sales; usually he puts this amount as a separate item on the bills his customers have to pay, but he can subtract from his tax liability all taxes he has paid to the sellers of the goods and machinery he needed for manufacturing. Thus, in effect, the tax he pays to the government is a percentage of the value he added to the product—hence the name of the tax.

c. Single-stage taxes, commonly called sales taxes, such as the sales tax most states in the United States are levying. For more detailed information on the mechanism of these taxes, see Organization for Economic Cooperation and Development, Report on Tax Adjustments Applied to Exports and Imports in OECD Member Countries (Paris, 1968), Chapters 1 to 5.

6. See Günter Schmölders, "Die Umsatzsteuern," p. 571. However, competition tends to be very strong in the food sector. This could mean that tax shifting is less likely in this case than, for example, in the automobile industry.

7. The revenue from sales taxes tripled in the decade from 1960 to 1970 (The New York Times, November 9, 1970, p. 28, col. 1). Tax rates are increasing permanently; they have now reached 8 percent in a few places (state and local tax combined); see 1971 Europäische Steuerzeitung 135 (1971). It is evident that at least some states try to catch up with European countries in this respect. (West Germany presently has a 11 percent VAT which was increased from 10 percent in 1968.)

8. See supra, note 3.

9. See Franklyn D. Holzman, Soviet Taxation, (Cambridge: Harvard University Press, 1962), pp. 87-95. In the Soviet Union, the turnover tax accounts for the bulk of the difference between the final price of a good and its production cost. Profits and profits tax are of considerably smaller importance. But in many respects, the turnover tax of the USSR cannot be compared with that of Western nations, just as prices and price relationships in a centrally planned economy are essentially different in nature from those in capitalist countries.

10. All special tax measures for internationally traded goods are in this book referred to as "border tax adjustments," regardless of their nature and effect. This broad definition is, however, not generally accepted. Many define "border tax adjustments" as those measures implementing the destination principle. Peter Buck Feller, "Mutiny Against the Bounty: An Examination of Subsidies, Border Tax Adjustments, and the Resurgence of Countervailing Duty Law," Law and Policy in International Business, I (1969), p. 50. The ordinary meaning of the words themselves suggests, however, that the label "border tax adjustments" would sensibly include also those measures necessary if the origin principle were adopted for a VAT or retail sales tax.

11. For further information, see Roger W. Rosendahl, "Border Tax Adjustments: Problems and Proposals," Law and Policy in International Business, II (1970), 85. At pp. 92-98, the legal history of the present GATT border tax rules is explored, especially with reference to earlier bilateral agreements concluded by the United States.

12. Cf. Milledge W. Weathers, "Some Implications of the GATT Rules Governing the Treatment of Domestic Taxes in International Trade: The Case of Germany Since the Currency Reform of 1948," National Tax Journal, XXIII (1970), 102.

13. Before the 1960s, France was the only country having a VAT. The mechanism of the VAT has, in simple terms, been explained above in note 5. The border adjustments under such a tax will be described in this footnote with reference to the German VAT law: Umsatzsteuergesetz (Mehrwertsteuer) of May 29, 1967 (CCH published an English-German text).

§4 (1) exempts deliveries to a foreign country from the 11 percent tax. §15 (2) explicitly says that nevertheless the entrepreneur who exports goods can deduct from his tax liability the tax charged to him by other entrepreneurs for deliveries. If the deductions exceed his tax liability, the difference is rebated to him. In simple terms, the government pays to the exporter the whole amount of the tax it has received for the exported product— that is, 11 percent of the price the exporter had to pay for it or its components. As to imports, §1(3) subjects them to the VAT. This "importation turnover tax" is technically levied like a tariff (§21). The entrepreneur who receives the imported good and resells it has to pay the VAT on his sale but can deduct the previously paid importation turnover tax (§15). The effect is that imported goods bear exactly the same VAT as domestically produced products: 11 percent of their price at each stage.

14. Judgment of June 16, 1966, 12 EUGH Rspr. 257. For an explanation of the questions of substantive law and of procedure involved here, the reader is referred to Eric Stein and Peter Hay, Law and Institutions in the Atlantic Area (Indianapolis-Kansas City-New York: Bobbs-Merrill, 1967), pp. 171-99. The term "self-executing" is explained at page 172.

15. Ulrich Everling, "Europaisches Gemeinschaftsrecht and nationales Recht in der praktischen Rechtsanwendung," 20 NJW 468 (1967).

16. Rolf Wägenbauer, "Das Verbot steuerlicher Diskriminierung nach dem EWG-Vertrag im Lichte der Rechtsprechung des Gerichtshofes," Europarecht, IV (1969), p. 20. West Germany has five separate judicial hierarchies. The fiscal courts (special courts for tax disputes) are one of them.

17. Article 109 (1).

18. Article 3 (1).
19. Judgment of March 5, 1958, 7 BVerfG 282.
20. Judgment of December 20, 1966, 21 BVerfG 12.
21. European Coal and Steel Community, High Authority: Report on the Problems Raised by the Different Turnover Tax Systems Applied Within the Common Market (Luxembourg, 1953), generally referred to as the "Tinbergen-Report."
22. The VAT had existed in France, in different forms and under different names, since 1937. Until 1968, it did not extend to the retail sector. Jean H. Rothstein, "Wandlungen im Steuerrecht Frankreichs," 15 AWD 209 (1969).
23. The Directives on Harmonization of Member State Turnover Tax Laws are reprinted (in unofficial translation) in 1 CCH Common Market Reporter, §311 et seq.
24. Tax News Service, (1971). Like European Taxation and Foreign Tax Law Weekly Bulletin, these reports are a convenient source for determining the latest changes in tax systems or rates. Facts in this discussion of the extension of VAT are taken from these services if not otherwise indicated, Part I, 9.
25. For a thorough treatment of this particular topic, see Clara K. Sullivan, The Tax on Value Added (New York: Columbia University Press, 1965).

CHAPTER 2

1. For details, the reader is referred to the materials in CCH Balance of Payments Reporter.
2. The following are examples of U.S. trade surpluses (in billions of dollars):
    1958: exports to EEC 2.8, imports from EEC 1.6.
    1966: exports 6.0, imports 4.4.
    1970: exports 9.0, imports 6.6.
European Taxation, X (1970), 182; 1972 Zeitschrift für Zolle und Verbrauchssteuern (1972), p. 19.
3. It will be shown in the following chapters that none of the lawyers who have taken up the subject have offered satisfactory policy conclusions. This is true of the two major treatises on GATT law (John H. Jackson, World Trade and the Law of GATT [Indianapolis, Ind.: Bobbs-Merrill, 1969]; and Kenneth W. Dam, The GATT, Law and International Economic Organization [Chicago: The University of Chicago Press, 1970]) as well as of the few contributions in legal periodicals.
4. CCH Balance of Payments Reporter §101, p. 109 (1968).
5. For example, in a televised interview with William F. Buckley, transmitted by many U.S. stations in the fall of 1970. See also European Taxation, Vol. X, No. 1 (1970), p. 83, with

respect to similar statements Stans made in Brussels, the capital of the EEC, in 1969.

6. The statistical information was gathered from certain companies for several products. In contrast to the report of the Organization for Economic Cooperation and Development (Report on Tax Adjustments Applied to Exports and Imports in OECD Member Countries [Paris, 1968]), where information was provided by the member countries and is of a theoretical (legal) kind, the numbers reveal the actual impact of border tad adjustments on business.

7. J. Frank Gaston and William J. J. Smith, Border Taxes and International Economic Competition, "Studies in Business Economics," #108 (The Conference Board) New York, pp. 21-56. The book has no date; the statistical information it contains is from 1967.

8. See, e.g., Peter Buck Feller, "Mutiny Against the Bounty: An Examination of Subsidies, Border Tax Adjustments, and the Resurgence of the Countervailing Duty Law," Law and Policy in International Business, I (1969), 54; and Helen Junz, "The Border Tax Issue Defined," in U.S. Congress, Joint Economic Committee, Subcommittee on Foreign Economic Policy, Issues and Objectives of U.S. Foreign Trade Policy: A Compendium of Statements (1967), p. 31.

9. So much has been written about tax shifting in the last decades and especially in the last few years that it is superfluous to deal with that subject here (only a definition is offered: the amount of shifting is the difference between the pre-tax price and the post-tax price of a good). The reader is referred to the OECD Report on Tax Adjustments . . . , §§156 and 157, which deal with the challenge, by modern economic theory, of the traditional assumptions regarding shifting of profit taxes; §158 et seq. sum up the results of major empirical studies on the shifting of profit taxes; §§128-49 consider the shifting of indirect taxes; and the bibliography contains references to some of the more important studies in this field.

It may be recalled that our definition of "indirect" and "direct" taxes (Chapter 1) rests upon a formal criterion—the way the tax is computed. The reader will now see why the older definition ("direct taxes are those taxes which are borne by the producer, indirect taxes those which are borne by the consumer") has intentionally been avoided here.

10. "One conclusion to be drawn from the economic literature is that full refund of an indirect tax constitutes in fact a subsidy to exports and therefore has the same distorting effect on international trade that any other export subsidy would have. A reciprocal conclusion is that an equalization charge on imported goods equal to

the full amount of an internal tax could have a protectionist effect"
(emphasis added). Dam, The GATT, Law and International Economic
Organization. The same view is held by eminent German tax economist Günter Schmölders: "The presently administered border
tax adjustments have the effect of a system of protective tariffs
and export subsidies. . . . The clear facts are today, that this
system . . . creates competitive distortions of international trade"
(emphasis added). Translated from Schmölders, Steuerliche
Wettbewerbsverzerrungen beim grenzüberschreitenden Warenverkehr im Gemeinsamen Markt (Köln-Berlin-Bonn-München:
Heymann, 1962),p. 47. In Chapter 4 of this study, an attempt is
made to show that this view is incorrect.

11. Gaston and Smith, Border Taxes and International Economic
Competition, p. 116.

12. See, e.g., Milton Leontiades, "The Logic of Border Taxes,"
National Tax Journal, XIX (1966), 182.

13. Hans Gerber, Steuerliche Probleme im zwischenstaatlichen
Warenverkehr und im Gemeinsamen Markt (Bern: Cosmos, 1963),
pp. 34-35.

14. E.g., by almost all participants in a discussion of economic
and legal experts reprinted in Schmölders, Steuerliche Wettbewerbsverzerrungen beim grenzüberschreitenden Warenverkehr im
Gemeinsamen Markt, pp. 29, 33, 40, 45. They all see the reason
for the "distortion" in the fact that in one country a much greater
part of the tax revenue is derived from indirect taxes than in the
other (the countries referred to were France and West Germany).

15. E.g., Jackson, World Trade and the Law of GATT, p. 298.

16. E.g., Feller, "Mutiny Against the Bounty," p. 52.

17. Schmölders, Steuerliche Wettbewerbsverrungen beim
grenzüberschreitenden Warenverkehr im Gemeinsamen Markt,
p. 22.

18. Richard A. Musgrave, one of the leading American tax
experts, is "inclined to this solution." Richard A. Musgrave, "Tax
Policy," Review of Economics and Statistics, XLVI (1964), 128.

19. Dam, The GATT, Law and International Economic Organization, p. 216; Jackson, World Trade and the Law of GATT, p. 302.

20. This thought has received much publicity since it was presented in Shoup, Carl S. Indirect and Direct Taxes and Their
Influence on International Trade, in compendium of papers on
excuse tax structure submitted to the Committee on Ways and
Means on June 15 and 16, 1964 (Washington, D.C.: U.S. Government
Printing Office, 1964), p. 59. It was apparently from there that it
found its way into the OECD Report on Tax Adjustments . . . .

21. However, a Working Party which in 1960 compiled a list
of measures considered to be subsidies for the purpose of Article

XVI of GATT stated that rebates of "direct" taxes were regarded as subsidies but those of "indirect" taxes were not. This Report was adopted by the Contracting Parties (9th Supp. BISD 185 [1961]). Even if the view were taken that such a Report could qualify the GATT rules, the statements following in the text would nevertheless apply, because (1) the Report speaks of "indirect taxes . . . levied on goods," and (2) the terms "indirect" and "direct" can be defined in accordance with the extent of tax shifting (see footnote 9, supra).

22. This is suggested by Jackson, World Trade and the Law of GATT, p. 298, footnote 19, in a cautious form ("An argument can be made that . . .").

23. Richard A. Musgrave, Fiscal Systems (New Haven, Conn.: Yale University Press, 1969), p. 277, footnote 9.

24. Cf. "Taxes and Non-Tariff Barriers: A Trade War in the Making?" European Taxation, Vol. X, No. 1 (1970), pp. 82-83. As to "defense" arguments, it should be noted that the official defense of the EEC against the public charges made by the United States was limited to the simple statement that the VAT did not discriminate between domestic and imported goods. Economic as well as legal scholars in the EEC countries are divided on the problem, as has already been indicated in connection with the tax dispute in the ECSC (Chapter 1). Therefore, many European writings could be used to support the American position.

25. See Gaston and Smith, Border Taxes and International Economic Competition, p. 6.

26. Naughton, "Connally Tells Senators Nixon Seeks Tax Reform," The New York Times, January 29, 1971, p. 1, col. 4. For another report on the study of a VAT see The New York Times, June 25, 1970, p. 67.

PART II INTRODUCTION

1. Trivial as this sounds, it has been neglected by many authors who have contributed their thoughts to the border tax problem. This is a main cause of the confusion that has accumulated and to which especially the OECD report, a principal source for all writers who have treated the subject since 1968, has added— Organization for Economic Cooperation and Development, Report on Tax Adjustments Applied to Exports and Imports in OECD Member Countries (Paris, 1968), p. 67 et seq.

CHAPTER 3

1. A thorough investigation of the efficiency aspects has commonly been neglected in the literature on the present border tax dispute. The leading study in this field, basic for all further investigations, is still J. Meade, The Theory of International

Economic Policy, Vol. II, Trade and Welfare, (London-New York-Toronto, Oxford University Press 1955). The opening discussion of this chapter partly deals with questions considered by Meade; however, the range of problems treated here is wider than in Meade's study, and the analytical approach also differs.

2. Other conditions are neglected here in that it can be shown that their fulfillment depends upon the two conditions mentioned; see ibid., pp. 51 ff.

3. Chameides, "Turnover Taxes and Tax Treaties," 22 BIFD 98 (1968).

4. The opinion that it makes no difference whether a general indirect tax follows the origin or the destination principle was already expressed by the Tinbergen Report—European Coal and Steel Community, High Authority: Report on the Problems Raised by the Different Turnover Tax Systems Applied Within the Common Market (Luxembourg, 1953), p. 24. It has been much more often refuted than accepted since, and three reasons may be given for this. First, the Report did not state its objectives very clearly. Apparently it considered only the most rational division of production (p. 23). Second, the Report lacked a detailed economic analysis; its language was too terse. Third, the phenomenon of tax shifting was not even mentioned, which led critics to the assumption that they had found a flaw: the neglect of modern views of tax shifting.

5. Special excises as a percentage of total tax revenue in 1967: France 15 percent, Italy 29 percent, West Germany 19 percent, Great Britain 27 percent. See 16 AWD 199 (1970), Table III.

6. See the rate tables in Haskins and Sells, Taxation in France (International Tax and Business Service, New York, 1970), p. 66; and 1971 Europäische Steuerzeitung (1971), p. 135.

7. Explanation of the desirability of equilibrium in the balance of payments is omitted here; any textbook on international economics discusses this subject. See Paul A. Samuelson, Economics, New York: McGraw-Hill (8th ed.; 1970), pp. 640-44, for a brief account ("Income and Unemployment Aspects of International Trade"). All countries regard equilibrium in the long run as one of the foremost goals of foreign economic policy. It is not, therefore, the desirability of avoiding a disequilibrium which is disputed, but the singling out of domestic tax changes as the sole justification of border adjustments. "Proposed Solutions," in Chapter 2, dealt with criticism of this kind.

8. The possible danger mentioned in the text is the main reason why Gottfried Haberler opposed a general levy/subsidy system in his famous, often-cited article "Import Taxes and Export Subsidies: A Substitute for the Realignment of Exchange Rates?" Kyklos, XX (1967), p. 22.

9. E.g., Robert E. Baldwin, <u>Nontariff Distortions of Inter-</u><u>national Trade</u> (Washington, D.C.: The Brookings Institution, 1970), pp. 19-22.

10. A system of the kind described in the example has been advocated by Harald B. Malmgren, a former Assistant Special Representative for Trade Negotiations to the U.S. President. Harald B. Malmgren, "The Border Tax Problem: Tax Harmonization in Europe and U.S. Business," <u>Canadian Tax Journal</u>, XVII (1969), p. 41. Border tax adjustments, Malmgren says, should be "a conscious, selective instrument of government economic policy." A similar proposal was made in 1970 by economist Baldwin, <u>Nontariff Distortions of International Trade</u>, p. 100.

11. Only "general" indirect taxes are considered, in that an increase of a selective tax on one or several goods will normally have only a minor impact on the balance of payments. If selective taxes with a broad coverage of goods, such as the Japanese commodity tax, are increased, the effect on the trade balance is in most respects comparable to that of an increase of a general tax. The reasoning presented here applies, therefore, to this case as well. The analysis in this section is only a brief sketch; the impact of general indirect taxes on the trade balance has been carefully scrutinized by Baldwin, <u>Nontariff Distortions of International Trade</u>, pp. 187-93 ("A Model for Analyzing General Indirect Taxes").

12. <u>Ibid</u>., p. 94 et seq. The hint at the Phillips curve is rather unconvincing because unemployment does not necessarily rise after the tax increase.

13. Richard A. Musgrave, "Tax Policy," <u>Review of Economics and Statistics</u>, XLVI (1964), p. 127: "It is unlikely that European indirect taxes did in fact lower money wages or retard increases. Most of these taxes existed throughout the period. . . . For Germany, lagging wage rates through most of the 1950's can be explained by other factors, just as the more recent increases have occurred in spite of the tax."

14. Walter Salant, "The Balance of Payments Deficit and the Tax Structure," <u>Review of Economics and Statistics</u>, XLVI (1964), p. 131. Salant argues that the initial price rise will entail a general wage increase in that some wages are directly tied to the consumer price index and other wages will be influenced by the latter's rise as well. "Western Europe, to the extent that it has made greater use of wage-raising indirect taxes than the U.S., has put itself at a competitive disadvantage" (p. 136).

15. The probability of a surplus is even smaller when trade with less-developed countries is considered. As a group, these countries do not increase their total foreign payments more than temporarily in the absence of an increase in their receipts. See <u>ibid</u>.

16. See, e.g., Musgrave, "Tax Policy," p. 128.

17. For his earlier view, see Richard A. Musgrave, The Incidence of the Tax Structure and its Effects on Consumption, Federal Tax Policy for Economic Growth and Stability, Joint Economic Committee, Subcommittee on Tax Policy (1956), p. 100.

18. British studies are cited in the Organization for Economic Cooperation and Development, Report on Tax Adjustments Applied to Exports and Imports in OECD Member Countries (Paris, 1968), pp. 163-67; American investigations in Baldwin, Nontariff Distortions of International Trade, p. 108.

19. OECD Report on Tax Adjustments . . . , §185, with reference to empirical research.

20. In Belgium, the "taxe sur la valeur ajoutée," introduced in 1971 in lieu of other indirect taxes, earned the nickname "tout va augmenter" (the same initials: TVA)—everything will go up. Norway substituted a VAT partly for other indirect taxes, partly for direct taxes, and found by the end of the year (1970) that the cost of living was up by more than 11 percent. Farnsworth, "Price Inflating Tax Angers Belgians," The New York Times, January 6, 1971, p. 2.

21. This term is used especially in civil law countries; see, e.g., Karl Teichner Internationales Steuerrecht (Stuttgart: Schäffer, 1967), or Ottmar Bühler, Prinzipien des internationalen Steuerrechts (Amsterdam: Internationales Steverdokumentationsbüro, 1964).

22. The question of the impact of indirect taxes (origin or destination principle) on international factor movements has not received much attention in economic literature. Meade's study of taxation in his Trade and Welfare rests on the classical assumption of international immobility of factors. Musgrave (in collaroba-tion with Peggy B. Richman) touches the topic in one of his studies of border tax adjustments. However, he considers a VAT of the "income-type"—a certain kind of VAT that is akin to an income tax and differs in this respect from the VAT that has conquered Western Europe. Referring briefly to a VAT of the consumption-type" (the one adopted in Europe) with border adjustments, he simply states that "the distorting effect (of the income tax) on capital flow will be reduced or absent." Labor movements are not considered. See Richard A. Musgrave and Peggy B. Richman, "Allocation Aspects, Domestic and International," in The Role of Direct and Indirect Taxes in the Federal Revenue System, Conference Report of the National Bureau of Economic Research and the Brookings Institution (Princeton, N.J.: Princeton University Press, 1964), p. 107. A few studies that originated in the EEC deal more thoroughly with the problem; see Olaf Sievert, Aussenwirtschaftliche Probleme steuerlicher Ausgleichsmassnahmen

für den internationalen Handel (Köln-Berlin-Bonn-München: Heymann, 1964), p. 89 et seq.; and Hans Möller, "Ursprungs-und Bestimmungs-landprinzip," Finanzarchiv, XXVII (1968), 385-458.

23. With respect to the international distribution of factors, economic theory can give indications regarding the most efficient solution (see Meade, The Theory of International Economic Policy, p. 51 et seq.). International capital movements that enhance efficiency are economically beneficial but they may be less desirable for at least one of the countries concerned in a political or social sense. Jean Jacques Servan-Schreiber's book The American Challenge (New York: Atheneum, 1968) provides examples for that. Migration of labor is connected with even more social and political implications. Any increase or reduction in world efficiency is necessarily of minor importance if compared to these social consequences. In this respect, the international movements of goods and those of factors differ greatly. The following statements of "efficiency costs" resulting from factor movements do not, therefore, represent final value judgments.

24. For an investigation of this problem, see Maria-Dolores Schulte, "The Economic Theory of the Destination Principle and the Origin Principle," in Institut International de Finances Publiques, Comparaison et harmonisation des systèmes des recettes publiques, particulièrement des systèmes fiscaux (York-Paris-Saarbrücken, (Institut International de Finances Publiques, 1966), pp. 217-47.

25. This statement reveals a kind of "black and white" thinking at which economists sometimes frown. The lawyer is more unscrupulous in this respect. It was observed earlier in the chapter that the destination principle is not apt to neutralize the effects of domestic tax changes completely. This is well demonstrated by the table provided by Helen Junz, "The Border Tax Issue Defined," in U.S. Congress, Joint Economic Committee, Subcommittee on Foreign Economic Policy, Issues and Objectives of U.S. Foreign Trade Policy: A Compendium of Statements (1967), p. 31, and by Richard A. Musgrave, Fiscal Systems (New Haven, Conn.: Yale University Press, 1969), p. 278. But observations of this kind must not lead to resignation. Objectionable as the destination principle may be, it is still superior to the origin principle. It may be noted, by the way, that the adoption of a "black and white" solution is not due to unwillingness to accept more differentiated rules, but to the fact that the exact effects of tax changes are unpredictable.

26. Adoption of the destination principle for selective indirect taxes is advocated in the Tinbergen Report (ECSC, High Authority: Report on the Problems Raised . . . at p. 25. The objective of this proposal is "the most rational division of production" (p. 23). The resulting harm to consumers is not mentioned.

According to Musgrave, in Fiscal Systems, "chances are
that production effects cause the more serious distortion" (p. 276).
"There is some basis for the view that international coordination
should be concerned primarily with production efficiency. As noted
before, potential losses from this side are likely to outweigh the
consumption burden" (p. 280).

27. See Baldwin, Nontariff Distortions of International Trade,
pp. 101-04 and 194-95.

28. Ibid., p. 195.

29. Moreover, this shakes Baldwin's conclusions regarding
general indirect taxes as well. He favors the destination principle
for these taxes mainly because he thinks that it is the best way to
deal with selective taxes and that a distinction between goods
subject to selective and general taxes would pose administrative
difficulties (ibid., p. 99). Inasmuch as his argument for the destination principle in the case of selective taxes is debatable, this
justification of the destination principle for general taxes no longer
carries weight.

30. Ibid., p. 109.

31. Musgrave, "Tax Policy," p. 128.

32. Ibid.

CHAPTER 4

1. See Paul A. Samuelson, Economics, (New York: McGraw-
Hill, 8th ed.; 1970), pp. 367-68.

2. This has been demonstrated by Robert E. Baldwin, Nontariff
Distortions of International Trade (Washington, D.C.: The Brookings
Institution, 1970), p. 191. His results were briefly stated in Chapter
3.

3. See, e.g., Kenneth W. Dam, The GATT, Law and Inter-
national Economic Organization (Chicago: The University of
Chicago Press, 1970), p. 216; John H. Jackson, World Trade and
the Law of GATT (Indianapolis, Ind.: Bobbs-Merrill, 1969), p. 302;
Helen Junz, "The Border Tax Issue Defined," in U.S. Congress,
Joint Economic Committee, Subcommittee on Foreign Economic
Policy, Issues and Objectives of U.S. Foreign Trade Policy, A
Compendium of Statements (1967), p. 35. The cited statements
are not very precise, however. Whereas this interpretation seems
to be most consistent with the words and the context, there remains
some doubt about the scheme the authors actually had in mind.

The practical difficulties mentioned in the text arise not
only from the uncertainty about the actual tax incidence but also
from the complexity of the administrative apparatus necessary
to apply such adjustments.

4. See Leland B. Yeager and David G. Tverck, Trade Policy and the Price System (Scranton, Pa.: International Textbook Company, 1967), p. 270.

5. Junz, "The Border Tax Issue Defined," p. 35.

6. B. Södersten, International Economics, (New York, Evanston, London: Harper & Row, 1970). "Discriminatory tariffs" are tariffs that apply only to exports from certain countries. Their adoption means abandonment of the most-favored-nation principle.

8. See, e.g., Dam, The GATT, Law and International Economic Organization, pp. 216-17.

9. Baldwin, Nontariff Distortions of International Trade, p. 5. In our terminology, this would be any measure that interferes with the conditions for utopian efficiency.

10. Ibid., p. 94.

11. See, e.g., Södersten, International Economics, pp. 13-22.

12. Gaston and Smith, Border Taxes and International Economic Competition, "Studies in Business Economics," #108 (The Conference Board), New York.

13. See Södersten, International Economics, p. 20. This is a simplified model, but the validity of the argumentation does not depend on the simplification.

14. Article VIII §3 of the International Monetary Fund Agreement: "No member shall engage in . . . any discriminatory currency arrangements or multiple currency practices except as authorized under this Agreement or approved by the Fund."

15. Therefore, Article VIII §3 of the IMF Agreement is not violated by a country that applies uniform border adjustments.

16. Jackson, World Trade and the Law of GATT, p. 302.

17. Schmolders, Günter, Steuerliche Wettbewerbsverzerrungen beim grenzüberschreitenden Warenverkehr im Gemeinsamen Markt (Köln-Berlin-Bonn-München: Heymann, 1962).

18. Similar arguments have been advanced in favor of tariff preferences for less-developed countries; see Harry G. Johnson, Economic Policies Towards Less Developed Countries (New York-Washington: Praeger, 1967), p. 185. It has been said that in less-developed countries private costs may even be higher than social costs and that it would be appropriate to give the products of these countries an artificial advantage over goods from developed nations in order to equalize for this difference. Tariff preferences would establish such an advantage.

19. This statement can be verified by scrutinizing the annual budgets of the United States and other countries. For an itemization of U.S. federal expenditure in 1970, see Samuelson, Economics, p. 143.

19. Jackson (World Trade and the Law of GATT, p. 298), after observing that GATT allows border tax adjustments only for indirect, not for direct taxes, states the following: "Thus, because of different tax structures and their relation to GATT, one country appears to have a considerable trade protection advantage over another." He links this to the protectionist effect resulting from a tariff: "Over the decades, as tariffs came down, . . . other protectionist devices became more prominent" (pp. 297-98). See also Roger W. Rosendahl, "Border Tax Adjustments: Problems and Proposals," Law and Policy in International Business, II (1970), 85: "If these assumptions (the traditional shifting assumptions) are not correct, export rebates and import charges would have a net protective effect vis-à-vis countries with a relatively greater reliance on direct taxation." (p. 108). (Emphasis in all cases added.)

21. Junz, "The Border Tax Issue Defined," p. 37.

22. Peter Buck Feller, "Mutiny Against the Bounty: An Examination of Subsidies, Border Tax Adjustments, and the Resurgence of the Countervailing Duty Law," (Law and Policy in International Business, I 1969), pp. 51-52.

23. E. J. Reig, "Type of Sales Tax Applied and the Problem of Tax Harmonization Within Common Market Areas," in Institut International de Finances Publiques, Comparaison et harmonisation des systèmes des recettes publiques, particulièrement des systèmes fiscaux (York-Paris-Saarbrücken, (Institut International de Finances Publiques, 1966), p. 191.

24. Reig refers to general sales taxes as well as to excise taxes; ibid., p. 188.

25. It is, therefore, misleading when Baldwin (Nontariff Distortions of International Trade, p. 84) writes: "When most foreign products enter Germany, for example, a tax of 11% is normally levied on the import plus duty value of the goods. On the other hand, the only German goods imported into the United States that are subject to charges of this kind are those comparatively few commodities on which a federal excise tax is levied domestically."

CHAPTER 5

1. See, e.g., Peter Weides, "Europäische Steuerrechtsangleichung," Juristenzeitung, XX (1965), 8-9, for a typical presentation of this argument. See also Chapter 2 of this book.

2. Fritz Neumark, "Grundsätze und Arten der Haushaltfuehrung und Finanzbedarfsdeckung," in Handbuch der Finanzwissenschaft, Vol. 1 (Tubingen: Mohr, 1952), p. 658.

3. The facts of this case are taken from Foreign Tax Law Weekly Bulletin, Vol. XXI, Nos. 25-26 (November 1970), pp. 6-7, and The New York Times, August 11, 1970, p. 8, col. 1.

4. For the facts of this discussion, see Tax Foundation, Retail Sales and Individual Income Taxes in State Tax Structures, New York (1962).

5. See, e.g., Freeman v. Hewit, 329 U.S. 249 (1946), where it was held that a state is precluded by the commerce clause from taxing an interstate sale, even if the state taxes intrastate sales.

6. Henneford v. Silas Mason Co., Inc. 300 U.S. 577 (1937).

7. Felt & Tarrant Mfg. Co. v. Gallagher, 306 U.S. 62 (1939).

8. U.S. Code 1964 Title 15, §§ 375-77.

9. Ibid., §376 (a) (2).

10. See The New York Times, May 12, 1971, p. 1, cols. 5-7.

11. 20 NYCRR 330. 1.

12. It is, however, not the only reason. Apart from the fiscal interests of the states, concern for the competitiveness of their businessmen has also been a force behind their striving for closing loopholes in the destination principle. See Cardozo's opinion in Henneford v. Silas Mason Co., Inc.

13. See Th. W. Vogelaar, "Steuerharmonisierung in der Europäischen Gemeinschaft," 16 AWD 198 (1970). Vogelaar is General Director in the Commission of the EEC.

14. Ibid., p. 201.

15. BGBl I, p. 1255 (1968). The law was repealed when, in 1969, the West German currency was revalued upward. Neither the 1961 revaluation nor the 1971 "floating" was preceded by a revaluation in the guise of a levy/subsidy system.

CHAPTER 6

1. See the list of GATT Participating Countries, John H. Jackson, World Trade and the Law of GATT (Indianapolis, Indiana: Bobbs-Merrill, 1969), p. 898 et seq.

2. See ibid., pp. 374-75.

3. Paul A. Samuelson, Economics, New York: McGraw-Hill (8th ed.; 1970), pp. 500, 506.

4. Rudolf Bernhardt, Die Auslegung voelkerrechtlicher Verträge (Köln-Berlin: Heymann, 1963), p. 22.

5. Ibid., p. 143 et seq.

6. See Articles 95 and 96 of the EEC Treaty.

7. 5 C.M.L.Rep. 97 (1966), at p. 109.

8. See, e.g., Wägenbauer, "Das Verbot steuerlicher Diskriminierung nach dem EWG-Vertrag im Lichte der Rechtsprechung des Gerichtshofes," Europarecht, IV (1969), 28.

9. For a detailed survey of many trading nations, see A. Milton Moore, Taxes and Exports (Toronto, Ontario: Canadian Tax Foundation 1963).

10. For a detailed description of the proposal, see the Treasury Department's Report to Congress, Foreign Tax Law Weekly Bulletin, Vol. XXI, No. 7/8 (July 1970), pp. 18-31.

11. See European Taxation, Vol. X, No. II (1970), p. 135.

12. See, e.g., Kenneth Dam, The GATT, Law and International Economic Organization (Chicago: The University of Chicago Press, 1970), pp. 118-19; Gerold Gerold Buschlinger, "Nichtzollbedingte Schranken gegen einen freien Warenaustausch," 12 AWD 185 (1966), at p. 191.

13. See Jackson, World Trade and the Law of GATT, p. 163 et seq.

14. The leading case is Bercut-Vandervoort v. United States, 46 CCPA Customs 28 (1958). See Dam, The GATT, Law and International Economic Organization, pp. 129-30.

15. Schieffelin v. United States, 424 F 2d 1369 (1970).

16. 400 U.S. 869 (1970).

17. "World Court Plea on Whisky Weighed," The New York Times, December 15, 1970, p. 63.

18. 91 S. Ct. 450 (1971).

19. Article 34 (1), Statue of the International Court of Justice.

20. If the statute has been enacted before a country's adoption of GATT obligations, the "Protocol of Provisional Application" and similar accession protocols have this effect. See Jackson, World Trade and the Law of GATT, pp. 106-10.

21. 26 U.S.C.A. § 7852 (d). This provision was crucial for the whisky cases. Paragraph 7852 (d) is not applicable to the provisions added by the 1962 Amendment to the Internal Revenue Code. In 1962, Congress apparently abandoned the idea that international treaties should supersede all domestic tax law. This policy change was heavily debated in the Senate. See Ottmar Bühler, Prinzipien des internationalen Steuerrechts (Amsterdam: Internationales Steverdokumentationsbüro, 1964), pp. 67-68.

22. Recently, the Fiscal Court of Hamburg (West Germany) ruled that Article III of GATT (taxation of imports) could not be regarded as a "general rule of international law"—Judgment of October 29, 1969, 16 AWD 91 (1970). However, the court based its decision mainly on the observation that many countries, especially the Soviet Union and Communist China, are not members of GATT. Hence, the court concluded, the rule is not "general." It is suggested that two important questions were overlooked by the judges. First, the fact that a nation is not a member of GATT does not necessarily mean that it does not apply the same border tax adjustment rules as the GATT countries. The taxation of internationally traded goods in East Germany, for example, has features similar to the GATT regulation. See Niels Reuter, Das

Recht der staatlichen Ausfuhrförderung (Gottingen: Institut für
Völkerrecht der Universität, 1959), p. 496. Second, taxation in
communist countries cannot be compared to that in Western
nations (see Chapter 1). It may well be that a rule that makes
sense only in free market countries is a "general" rule when it is
adopted by the great majority of these countries.

23. See, e.g., the judgment of the West German Bundesgericht-
shof 19 NJW 877 (1966).

24. For the Countervailing Duty Law cf the United States, see
§303 of the Tariff Act of 1930 (19 U.S.C.A. §1303). The Countervailing Duty Law of the European Economic Community is contained
in Council Regulation 459/68 (CCH Common Market Reports 3883).

APPENDIX

Notes to Appendix

1. See, e.g., Bo Sodersten, International Economics (New York-
Evanston-London: Harper and Row, 1970), pp. 342-46. This is
the model that shows the two "costs" of a tariff (neglecting its
secondary effects) in the form of two triangles: the "production
loss" and the "consumption loss." Other geometric representations
of the two losses (or the advantages of free trade, which mirror
them) are also possible; see, e.g., ibid., p. 38 (using the production
possibility curve of the tariff-imposing country). They, too, could
be used to explain the tax problem, but the first figure seems to
present the case most clearly. Figure 1, which is used for the
case of an imported product, is a direct adaption from the model
that usually explains the effect of a tariff, whereas Figure 2 (for
the case of exported goods) is only indirectly related to it. Figure
3 is, like Figure 1, adapted from a model used in basic tariff
theory.

2. The best compromise between the two policies was investigated by J. Meade, in The Theory of International Economic
Policy, Vol. II of Trade and Welfare (London-New York-Toronto,
Oxford University Press, 1955) in two different contexts: pp. 226-40
deal with the issue of how interference with free trade can redress
the negative effect of domestic divergences between marginal
values and costs on the world economy, whereas pp. 193-99 consider the "second-best" way of raising revenue when the "first-
best," a certain impractical poll tax, is not feasible. Surprisingly,
the results differ in the two cases, which is due to the fact that in
the first one Meade tacitly assumes the terms of trade to be un-
alterable, whereas in the second one he considers all sorts of
elasticities. Whereas Meade's basic conclusions are not debatable,

his reasoning is very complex and sometimes equivocal, and it is only the translation of his considerations into the simple geometric models attempted here that makes the problem clear even to the noneconomist.

3. For a brief explanation of the term "consumer surplus," see Paul A. Samuelson, Economics New York: McGraw-Hill (8th ed.; 1970), pp. 417-18. The meaning of "consumption cost" or "consumption loss" is, in the context of tariff theory, elaborated by Södersten, International Economics, pp. 344-45.

4. It was mentioned in note 1 that the production possibility curve of the taxing country could be used to explain tax problems. This was done by Robert E. Baldwin, Nontariff Distortions of International Trade (Washington, D.C.: The Brookings Institution, 1970), p. 196. Baldwin uses this model merely in order to show that it cannot be established whether the origin principle or the destination principle is superior with respect to economic welfare, provided that no specific assumptions (in his case, assumptions concerning the shape of the community indifference curves) are made. He does not draw any further conclusion from the figures he provides. Instead, he tackles the problem of selective indirect taxes in a different way, which is described (and criticized) in Chapter 3 in an analysis of his view of "international equity."

5. For a proof of this presumption, see Meade, The Theory of International Economic Policy, p. 195.

6. Ibid., pp. 197-98.

SELECTED BIBLIOGRAPHY

Baldwin, Robert E. Nontariff Distortions of International Trade. Washington, D.C.: The Brookings Institution, 1970.

Buschlinger, Gerold. "Nichtzollbedingte Schranken gegen einen freien Warenaustausch," Aussenwirtschaftsdienst des Betriebsberaters (AWD), XII (1966), 185-92.

Dam, Kenneth W. The GATT, Law and International Economic Organization. Chicago: The University of Chicago Press, 1970.

European Coal and Steel Community. High Authority: Report on the Problems Raised by the Different Turnover Tax Systems Applied Within the Common Market. Luxembourg, 1953.

Feller, Peter Buck. "Mutiny Against the Bounty: An Examination of Subsidies, Border Tax Adjustments, and the Resurgence of the Countervailing Duty Law," Law and Policy in International Business, I. (1969), 17-76.

Gaston, J. Frank, and William J. J. Smith. Border Taxes and International Economic Competition. "Studies in Business Economics," New York, #108. The Conference Board.

Gerber, Hans. Steuerliche Probleme im zwischenstaatlichen Warenverkehr und im Gemeinsamen Markt. Bern: Cosmos, 1963.

Jackson, John H. World Trade and the Law of GATT. Indianapolis, Ind.: Bobbs-Merrill, 1969.

Junz, Helen. "The Border Tax Issue Defined," in U.S. Congress, Joint Economic Committee, Subcommittee on Foreign Economic Policy, Issues and Objectives of U.S. Foreign Trade Policy: A Compendium of Statements (1967), p. 35.

Leontiades, Milton. "The Logic of Border Taxes," National Tax Journal, XIX (1966), 173-83.

Lindholm, Richard W. "National Tax System and International Balance of Payments," National Tax Journal, XIX (1966), 163-72.

_____. "Some Value-Added Tax Impacts on the International Competitiveness of Producers," Journal of Finance, XXIII (1968), 659-65.

Malmgren, Harald B. "The Border Tax Problem: Tax Harmonization in Europe and U. S. Business," Canadian Tax Journal, XVII (1969), 34-42.

Meade, J. The Theory of International Economic Policy. Vol. II, Trade and Welfare. London-New York-Toronto: Oxford University Press, 1955.

Mesenberg, Heinz. "Steuerstruktur und zwischenstaatlicher Wettbewerb," Deutsches Steuerrecht (1965), pp. 59-64.

Möller, Hans. "Ursprungs-und Bestimmungslandprinzip," Finanzarchiv, XXVII (1968), 385-458.

Musgrave, Richard A. Fiscal Systems. New Haven, Conn.: Yale University Press, 1969.

_____. "Tax Policy," Review of Economics and Statistics, XLVI (1964), 127.

Musgrave, Richard A., and Peggy B. Richman. "Allocation Aspects, Domestic and International," in The Role of Direct and Indirect Taxes in the Federal Revenue System. Conference Report of the National Bureau of Economic Research and the Brookings Institution. Princeton, N.J.: Princeton University Press, 1964.

Organization for Economic Cooperation and Development. Report on Tax Adjustments Applied to Exports and Imports in OECD Member Countries. Paris, 1968.

Rosendahl, Roger W. "Border Tax Adjustments: Problems and Proposals," Law and Policy in International Business, II (1970), 85-146.

Salant, Walter. "The Balance of Payments Deficit and the Tax Structure," Review of Economics and Statistics, XLVI (1964), 131.

Schmölders, Günter. Steuerliche Wettbewerbsverzerrungen beim grenzüberschreitenden Warenverkehr im Gemeinsamen Markt. Köln-Berlin-Bonn-München: Heymann, 1962.

Schulte, Maria-Dolores. "The Economic Theory of the Destination
    Principle and the Origin Principle," in Institut International de
    Finances Publiques, Comparaison et harmonisation des systèmes
    des recettes publiques, particulièrement des systèmes fiscaux,
    pp. 217-47. York-Paris-Saarbrücken: Institut International de
    Finances Publiques, 1966.

Shoup, Carl S. Indirect and Direct Taxes and Their Influence on
    International Trade. In compendium of papers on excise tax
    structure submitted to the House Committee on Ways and Means
    on June 15 and 16, 1964. Washington, D.C.: U.S. Government
    Printing Office, 1964. P. 57.

Sievert, Olaf. Aussenwirtschaftliche Probleme steuerlicher Ausgleichs-
    massnahmen für den internationalen Handel. Köln-Berlin--
    Bonn-München: Heymann, 1964.

Tax Foundation. Tax Harmonization in Europe and U.S. Business:
    New York, 1968.

Weathers, Milledge W. "Some Implications of the GATT Rules Gov-
    erning the Treatment of Domestic Taxes in International Trade:
    The Case of Germany Since the Currency Reform of 1948,"
    National Tax Journal, XXIII (1970), 102-11.

ABOUT THE AUTHOR

MICHAEL FREIHERR VON STEINAECKER was born in Tuernitz, Austria, and holds dual citizenship in Austria and West Germany. He studied law at the universities of Vienna and Hamburg before graduating as a Rechtsreferendar from Munich University. He earned his Doctorate of the Science of Law (J.S.D.) at Cornell University. As a student he was awarded several fellowships including International Legal Studies (Cornell) and a Cornell Graduate Fellowship. Dr. von Steinaecker is now in the Landgericht, or provincial law court, in Traunstein, West Germany.